CRAFTING WITH
Digital Cutting
Machines

Design/project contributors: Tabitha Carty and Amelia Johanson

ISBN 978-1-4971-0154-8

Library of Congress Control Number: 2021944627

To learn more about the other great books from Fox Chapel Publishing, or to find a retailer near you, call toll-free 800-457-9112 or visit us at *www.FoxChapelPublishing.com*.

We are always looking for talented authors. To submit an idea, please send a brief inquiry to acquisitions@foxchapelpublishing.com.

Printed in China
First printing

CRAFTING WITH
Digital Cutting Machines

MACHINES, MATERIALS, DESIGNS, AND PROJECTS

LIBBY ASHCRAFT

FOX CHAPEL
PUBLISHING

Contents

60

66

74

82

85

90

Introduction

Welcome to the world of digital cutting machines. You are going to have so much fun learning about digital cutting machines and crafting that a digital cutter is sure to become an essential part of your sewing and crafting room—if it isn't already! Whether you know exactly what you want to make or are looking for ideas and inspiration to get the most out of your digital cutting machine, immersed in the pages of this book is exactly where you want to be.

With a few exceptions, all the projects that follow can be created using any digital cutter, and learning how to use your machine and what it can do is just as important as what you can make with it. There is a myriad of information available on paper crafting with digital cutters, but I'm always surprised by how little you can find on cutting fabrics and other materials. Few digital-cutting crafters know and use their machines' full capacity. In this book, I will introduce you to three popular machine models. Along with descriptions of the machines' components and features, I've included a synopsis of the blades, tools, mats, and other accessories used with each one.

I've found that, once you know the basics, the best way to broaden your knowledge is to be a "hands-on" learner and just create. It is my hope that, in doing so, you expand your personal library of techniques and skills to get the most from your digital cutting machine.

All the designs in this book are available as scalable vector graphic (SVG) files for you to download and use however you choose. If you love a particular project but envision it with a different design, there are endless designs online that you can purchase and download. Likewise, if a particular material (often referred to as a "medium") isn't to your liking, give it a try anyway—you may be surprised to find something you really love! You'll see that digital cutting machines truly do offer endless creative possibilities.

Let's get started!

Pay attention to my tips and tricks throughout the book. Trust me—I learned the hard way!

Digital Cutting Inspiration

You can download the SVG design files for the projects shown on pages 8–13 at *https://foxchapelpublishing.com/news/digital-cutting*. SVG files are scalable, allowing you to enlarge or reduce the design as desired in your cutting machine's software. Step-by-step instructions are included in this book for the pillows (pages 74 and 86), fox apron (pages 60), gift bags (pages 90), quilt (pages 66), and ornaments (pages 82). For advice on specific techniques, such as using transfer tape, using rhinestone flock, weeding, or etching, refer to Techniques to Know, starting on page 44.

Felt-Lettered Pillows: Lend a little pizzazz to a bedroom, dorm room, or family room by adding words to decorative pillows. Use the downloadable block letters (Alphabet_Pillow.svg) to create whatever words suit your fancy. Smaller letters, approximately 3⅝" (9.2cm) tall, are ideal for the 12" x 20" (30.5 x 50.8cm) pillow form shown. Cut the letters from felt, then cut the same letters from adhesive bond and apply to the back of each letter. Use a strong-tack mat to cut the felt and a light-tack mat with mirror-image function for cutting the adhesive bond. Turn to page 74 for full instructions for making these felt-lettered pillows.

"Create" Sign: Decorate your creative space with this inspirational message. Start with a ½" (1.3cm) plank, approximately 48" tall x 6" wide (1.2m x 15.2cm). Sand it, then stain it the color of your choice. Cut 4½" (11.4cm) letters from the file Alphabet_Create.svg in a mix of adhesive vinyl colors using the light-tack mat, then weed and position the letters on your prepared board with the aid of transfer tape. Pull the transfer tape at an angle, not with the grain of the wood, to prevent the stain and grain from being pulled up by the transfer tape. Letters start 6" (15.2cm) from the top of the board, with 1" (2.5cm) between each letter. **Tip:** Use painter's tape to space the letters evenly.

Hexagonal Cork Wall Hangings: Add silhouettes to purchased cork hexagons (or cut your own hexagons on your machine) to spice up your sewing room. Using the Wall Hanging downloadable designs, cut the silhouettes on a standard mat from 12" (30.5cm) square permanent vinyl sheets and a small piece of glitter vinyl. When cutting pieces to layer, make sure to use alignment boxes at the top of each cut for precise placement. Weed, then use transfer tape to pull up and place each layer. **Tip:** Command™ strips work very well for hanging these pieces.

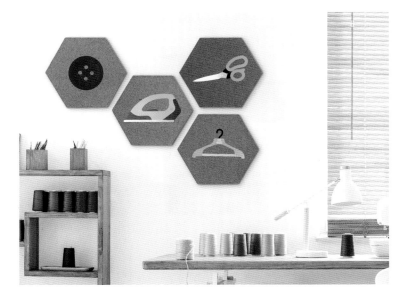

Faux-Suede Hexagon Pillow: Sensuede® is a win-win fabric for digital cutting. It not only cuts like a breeze, but this quality, fabric-weight faux suede won't fray, so you are left with a clean raw edge without the need for any stabilizers, seam sealants, or webbing. Use the standard-tack mat and cut approximately 25 hexagons. Turn to page 86 for step-by-step pillow instructions.

Raw-Edge Appliqué Owl Quilt: Raw-edge appliqué and digital cutting go hand in hand, as you can see in this adorable owl design. Be sure to cut on a strong-tack or standard-grip mat and test-cut to check your settings. Back your layer-cake squares with Heat n Bond® double-sided fusible web if you don't want your raw edges to fray slightly. If you like the frayed look, prepare your squares with Terial Magic first for clean cuts, then apply slightly smaller pieces of fusible web individually. Turn to page 66 for step-by-step instructions on making this quilt.

Quilt Lover's Phone Case: A fun little way to share your love of quilting with the world, or a perfect gift for a quilting friend, this quilt-block phone case is a beginner-level project that you can make on your lunch break. The key to making this quick-and-easy project long-lasting is the laminate layer, which is detailed on page 46.

"Dream" Canvas Art: The sky's the limit when you start with a purchased hanging blank. Shown here is a 16" x 21" (40.6 x 53.3cm) canvas embellished with a 9" (22.9cm)–wide foil heat transfer vinyl (HTV) word ("Dream") encircled by a wreath of dark green, light green, and patterned HTV flowers and leaves. Duplicate approximately six to eight of each flower and stem design in multiple sizes from 1" to 3" (2.5 to 7.6cm). Apply the word in the center and lightly trace around a 12" (30.5cm)–diameter dinner plate to create a wreath guideline before auditioning each piece. **Tip:** Remember that patterned HTV is cut without mirroring, while regular HTV should be mirrored.

Etched Glass Button Jar: Every crafter has a stash of buttons. Buttons of all shapes, sizes, and colors look quite pretty all tossed together, so why not take advantage of your digital-cutting prowess and etch a cool glass container to keep your buttons on display? For etching basics, turn to page 48, and remember that, in this project, you'll be weeding away what you would normally keep because those areas will be etched with etching cream.

Children's Fox Apron: Little people will love protecting their clothes from kitchen or art-room messes with this precious fox apron. Apply Heat n Bond® double-sided fusible web to your fabrics before cutting, and position fabrics on a strong-tack or standard-tack mat for cutting. The sizes of your cut pieces depend on the size of the apron. Turn to page 60 for instructions on adding fox details to a pre-purchased apron.

Holiday Ornaments: Create your own vintage-look ornaments with your electronic cutter and felt. This project is an easy twist on a classic craft. These ornaments finish around 6" to 7" (15.2 to 17.8cm), and the mitten ornament (see photo on page 41) is adorned with a snowflake detail cut from white HTV. Cut two of each piece for each ornament to create a front and a back. Turn to page 82 for step-by-step instructions to make tree (shown), mitten, and gift-box felt ornaments.

Rhinestone Tote: Plain tote bags are easy to come by, and you can make yours dazzling with an electronic cutter and rhinestone flock. Cutting rhinestone flock creates perfectly sized design "holes" that capture your rhinestones in a pattern, which you then transfer with rhinestone transfer tape to your project. Turn to page 50 for more detailed instructions on using rhinestones and rhinestone flock.

Drawstring Gift Bags: Add some flair to fabric drawstring gift bags to celebrate any event. Cut the pieces from a selection of patterned, solid, and glitter HTV, sizing so they finish 2" to 3" (5.1 to 7.6cm) from the edges of your bag. Turn on the mirror function for your words according to your machine. Use heat-resistant transfer tape because you will press your words and shapes to the fabric surface. Turn to page 90 for step-by-step instructions on making your own drawstring bags.

Leather Earrings: Feel like you need a new pair of earrings . . . or three? Combine shapes cut from leather or faux leather with jewelry findings to create unique, lightweight earrings in a snap. Cutting this material requires a strong-tack mat, and it can be cut with either a standard blade or a kraft blade, depending on your cutter. Embellish with a cut of HTV if desired, and cut the top leather pieces about ½" to 1" (1.3 to 2.5cm) smaller than the main earring cuts.

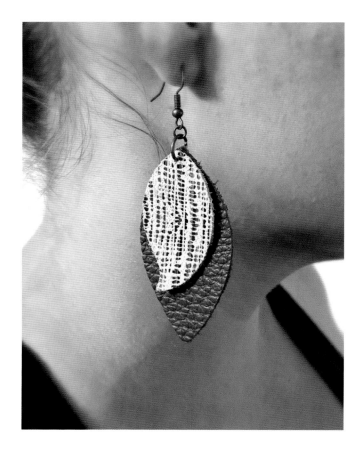

Glossary

It's important that you familiarize yourself with some of the terminology you'll encounter throughout this book as well as in many digital-cutting instructions and tutorials. I know you're eager to jump right into the projects, but please take some time to read through the information that follows. No one wants to stop in the middle of a project to figure out what the instructions mean!

Note: Some of the definitions mention the Silhouette Cameo®, Brother ScanNCut, or Cricut® digital cutting machines. These digital cutters are discussed in more detail in the next chapter.

Adhesive vinyl

Adhesive vinyl: Vinyl with adhesive backing; designed for use on hard surfaces.

Alignment: The orientation of lines of text in relation to the page. *Left alignment* means the text is aligned with the left margin, *right alignment* means that text is aligned with the right margin, and *centered* means that the line of text is centered between the two margins.

Autoblade: A type of blade in which the depth of the blade exposed for cutting automatically adjusts. With the Cameo and Cricut machines, Autoblade depth is controlled by software. The ScanNCut measures a blank area of the mat, then the area on the mat where the material is placed, and adjusts the blade depth accordingly.

Blade: The tool that cuts the media.

Blade housing: The part of the cutter where the blade is placed for cutting. It holds the blade in place for accurate cutting.

Blank: The medium on which the design is placed. It can be a hard surface, like a cup, acrylic, or wood, or it can be fabric, a garment, or another type of soft good.

Bounding box: The "box" around a selected design or group of designs. It usually has small squares that you can use to resize the design as well as a rotation handle that enables you to rotate the design.

CanvasWorkspace: Software (available both online and as a download) used with the ScanNCut for creating and editing designs.

Character spacing: The distance between characters in a word.

Cricut Design Space: Software used with Cricut cutters to create and cut designs.

Dual carriage: A feature that enables a digital cutting machine to perform two functions without having to switch out the drawing, cutting, etching, or other tools. Some Cricut cutters and some Silhouette cutters have a dual carriage, which means you can use two different tools in the same project. In the Silhouette Cameo® 4 series, the second holder in the dual carriage is for specialty blades and tools.

Etching: The process of creating a permanent design by scratching or cutting into the surface of a blank with either a special blade or a chemical etching cream. Not all digital cutters are designed for etching with a blade.

Etching cream: A product used with a stencil to etch permanent designs into glass, mirrors, or slate.

Font: Typeface files that are installed in your computer for use in various applications, including your design software. Fonts are either TTF (TrueType font) or OTF (OpenType font). OTFs are preferred because they support more special characters (glyphs) than TTFs.

Glyphs: Special characters found in some fonts that add swirls, curls, and other additions to text.

Group: Two or more elements combined in a design. Grouped elements can be moved, sized, or otherwise edited as one object.

Heat transfer vinyl (HTV): Vinyl designed to be applied to fabric using either a heat press or an iron. HTV has a shiny carrier sheet and is cut in reverse, so designs need to be mirrored when cutting HTV. Printed HTV requires a separate carrier sheet and is not mirrored when cut. HTV requires the correct time, temperature, and pressure, as specified by the manufacturer, to adhere well.

Justification: The spacing of a line of text so that it is aligned with both the left and right margins.

Line spacing: The space between lines of text within a text box.

Mat: A flat, gridded surface on which media is positioned to be cut. Mats are tacky, which helps hold the material in place for accurate cutting. Mats come in different sizes and levels of stickiness.

Offset: A duplicate of an object that is used either to create a multi-layer effect or to create cut lines around print-and-cut designs. An external offset is larger than the original, and an internal offset is smaller than the original.

Print and cut: The process of printing a design using an inkjet or laser printer and then cutting around the design for use in a craft project.

Press pillow: A foam-filled pillow covered with Teflon™ material. It is placed under or inside an item like a garment or a tote bag when pressing to raise the area to be pressed.

TIP In some projects, seams and straps can keep the design area from receiving even pressure, and uneven pressure can cause vinyl to not adhere properly. Using a press pillow solves this problem. I've included instructions for making your own press pillow on page 54.

Heat transfer vinyl

Rhinestone flock: Special material used to cut a rhinestone template. It is thicker than vinyl and has an adhesive backing. It comes on a paper carrier sheet onto which it can be placed for storage after use.

Rhinestone transfer tape: Heat-resistant adhesive transfer tape used to lift rhinestones from a rhinestone flock template. This transfer tape remains on the project during pressing.

Silhouette Studio: Software that allows you to create and cut designs using a Silhouette Cameo, Portrait, or Curio.

Squeegee: A flat, blade-like tool that helps vinyl adhere to transfer tape or the blank. It is used to smooth vinyl onto a blank, remove air bubbles, and apply laminate to vinyl.

Test cut: A small cut used to check settings before cutting an entire design. The Silhouette and ScanNCut have built-in test cuts.

Transfer tape: Tape used to remove adhesive vinyl from its backing and then place the vinyl on a blank.

Weed: To remove excess vinyl or fabric from around the cut design.

Weeding tool: A pick-like tool with a sharp point. It is used to help lift vinyl from its carrier sheet during weeding, and it can also help remove small pieces of fabric and paper from a cut.

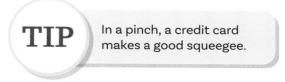

TIP In a pinch, a credit card makes a good squeegee.

Digital Cutting Machines

Before we explore the three top-selling digital cutting machines—Silhouette Cameo, Brother ScanNCut, and Cricut—and learn about the blades, mats, and other tools used with these machines, we'll start with a general overview of the digital cutting machine. Next, descriptions of the Cameo, ScanNCut, and Cricut can help you decide which one of these machines best meets your needs. Even if you already own one of these models, read on. You never know—you might discover a feature you haven't tried yet or a blade or tool you didn't know existed. The more you know, the more you'll enjoy your machine.

Digital cutting machines are popular with crafters for their versatility with many materials and types of projects.

An Overview

First and foremost, a digital cutting machine is used to cut shapes and letters with precise edges from all sorts of materials. If you think of a digital cutter in relation to a computer's printer, where a printer would lay down ink, a digital cutting machine will cut though a chosen medium. Traditional, manual models, which I mention only briefly, use rollers, cutting plates, and pressure to cut to exact specifications. With a manual machine, you build a "sandwich" by positioning a steel die (essentially the template) and the chosen material between a top and bottom cutting plate. As soon as home digital cutting merged with computer technology, however, electronic digital cutters revolutionized the craft. Where digital cutting was once the domain of the paper crafter, it's now becoming increasingly popular with quilters, jewelry makers, sewing and design enthusiasts, and general crafters alike.

Today's computer-savvy crafters now enjoy the option of connecting their electronic machines to their laptops, their desktops, or even their phones to expand their creative possibilities. Digital cutters do not use steel dies, nor do the newest versions use cartridges (as some earlier models do), but instead rely on web-based or downloaded software. A digital cutter contains blade holders, into which various blades are inserted, and its cutting is controlled by a computer. The modern digital cutter is designed to cut paper, fabrics, faux leather, stickers, specialty papers, cork, felt, craft metals, and more. Instead of building a "sandwich," you place your materials on a mat, which you load into the machine, and designs are cut digitally. Depending on your cutter, some materials, like vinyl, can even be cut without a mat because they come with a carrier sheet attached.

Some basic components and concepts apply to all electronic digital cutting machines. In general, a digital cutter will come with a mat, a blade, a power cord, and a USB cable (if needed). Depending on the brand and bundle you purchase, your machine may come with additional items.

The mat included with your machine is a standard mat that you can use with a wide variety of media. Additional mats that you can purchase separately include light tack (less sticky) and strong tack (very sticky). Light-tack mats are great for lightweight materials and paper. Strong-tack mats are designed to use with fabric and heavier materials like leatherette and marine vinyl.

Newer digital cutters come with an autoblade. The depth of the autoblade automatically adjusts based on your software settings or, in the case of the ScanNCut, the depth measurement it takes before cutting. Specialty blades are available for each of the digital cutters, and each blade is designed for a specific function or for specific types of media. Examples include rotary blades for cutting fabric and deep-cut blades for cutting thicker materials. These blades are often machine-specific and are not interchangeable even within different models made by the same brand.

You may come across the term "dual carriage" frequently in reference to the newer digital cutter models. A dual-carriage machine allows you to use two tools in the same project. In some machines, for example, you can use a pen in one side and a blade in the other. In other machines, the second carriage is designed only for specific specialty tools.

> **Note:** The blades pictured in this section for each of the digital cutting machines are not all-inclusive lists, and new blades are introduced for these machines frequently.

Silhouette Cameo

The Silhouette Cameo 4 features a 12" (30.5cm) cutting width, the Cameo 4 Plus has a 15" (38.1cm) cutting width, and the Cameo 4 Pro has a 24" (61cm) cutting width. All Cameo 4 models feature dual carriage: Tool 1 is designed for use with the included autoblade and several other non-specialty blades, and Tool 2 has increased power and is used with a variety of specialty blades that can be purchased separately. Some blades use the settings in Silhouette Studio software to adjust the depth of the blade, while others require manual adjustment. A set of adapters is included with the machine to allow you to use a wide range of blades.

The Cameo 4 models also feature matless cutting and can cut designs up to 60 feet (18.3m) in length. The built-in roller feeder makes these cutters perfect for longer projects.

The Cameo's Print and Cut technology lets you print designs and then accurately cut around them. PixScan™ technology takes this a step further, allowing "fussy cutting" of materials placed on the PixScan mat. Newer Cameo models are Bluetooth® enabled.

Silhouette Studio software is a download from the Silhouette America website (www.silhouetteamerica.com). With the free basic version, you can open designs or artwork, create your own artwork with the included tools, add text, and send your cut job to the cutter. Three upgrades can be purchased for this software: Designer Edition, Designer Edition Plus, and Business Edition. Each level unlocks additional tools and features. The upgrades are a one-time purchase.

At the basic level, Silhouette Studio reads STUDIO, DXF, JPG, BMP, and PNG files. The STUDIO and DXF files are cut-ready, and the JPG, BMP, and PNG files need to be traced to create cut lines. Designer Edition allows you to open SVG files, which are cut-ready and available from many sources. It also opens PDF files and converts the design elements to cut files. Designer Edition Plus allows you to open some embroidery files (PES, DST, EXP, JEF, and XXX) for cutting appliqué pieces. Business Edition also opens AI, CDR, and EPS files, and it allows you to save files as SVG files for use with other cutters.

The Silhouette Design Store features thousands of designs and fonts that are ready to use with Silhouette machines. You can also download fonts and SVG versions of designs (if available) for use with any other digital cutting machine or graphics software. Designs and fonts purchased through the store are yours to keep. A subscription is not required, but several subscription levels are available.

TIP

Some blades do not adjust automatically, so you will need to adjust them yourself. The software will indicate the recommended blade depth but does not make the adjustment. Also, the settings will vary as you cut different materials and as your blades become duller. This changes with every brand of material, every type of material you cut, the blade you use, and how long you have used the blade, so there is no magical number. Always do a test cut first, starting with the recommended setting.

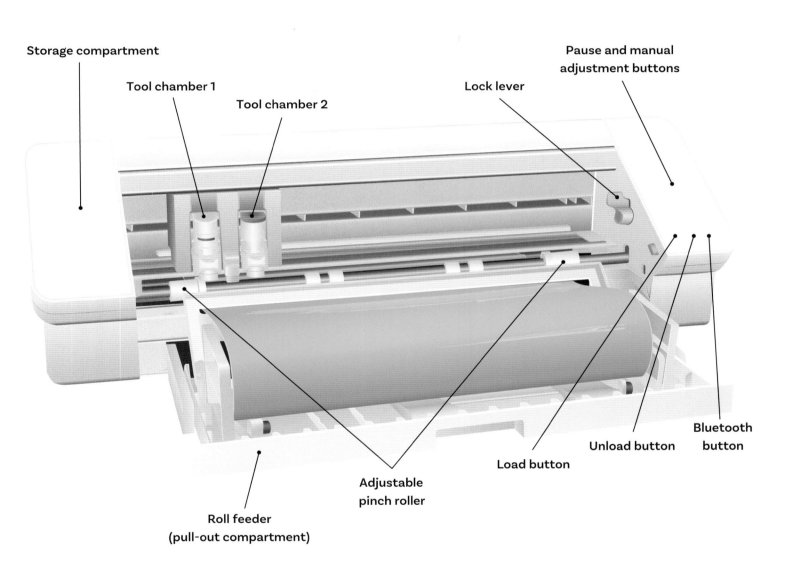

Storage compartment

Tool chamber 1

Tool chamber 2

Lock lever

Pause and manual adjustment buttons

Bluetooth button

Unload button

Load button

Adjustable pinch roller

Roll feeder (pull-out compartment)

Cameo 4 Blades and Tools

Ratchet blade

- Cuts all types of media, including paper, cardstock, fabric, sticker paper, HTV and adhesive vinyl, and specialty materials

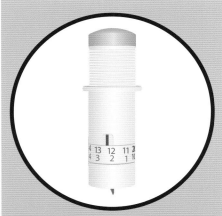

Premium blade

- Cuts all types of media, including paper, cardstock, fabric, sticker paper, HTV and adhesive vinyl, and specialty materials

Deep-cut blade

- 2mm blade; cuts through thicker materials, such as thick cardstock, craft foam, and specialty materials

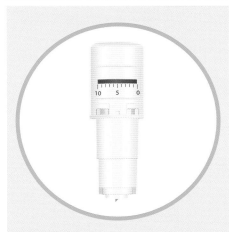

Autoblade

- Included with Cameo 4 models; cuts paper, cardstock, sticker paper, HTV and adhesive vinyl, fabric, and specialty materials

- Automatic adjustment based on settings selected in Silhouette Studio

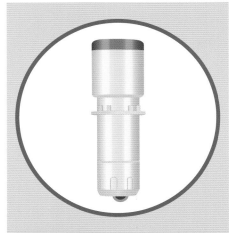

Rotary blade

- Rolling blade; cuts materials such as cotton fabric, leather, wool, felt, and crepe paper

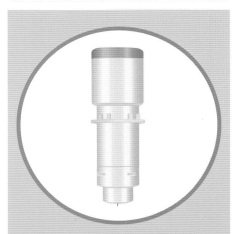

Punch tool

- Punches weeding points, for either positive or negative spaces, on vinyl and heat transfer projects

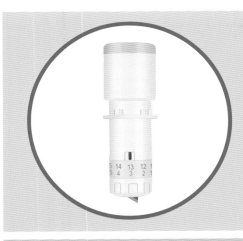

2mm kraft blade

- Cuts materials such as leather, craft foam, acetate, and chipboard

3mm kraft blade

- Cuts materials such as leather, craft foam, acetate, and chipboard using the Cameo 4's increased clearance

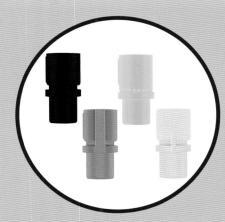

Tool adapter set

- Allows Cameo 4 users to use tools that were originally designed for earlier models; included with Cameo 4 machines
- Black adapter: Use with ratchet and fabric blades, new-style premium blade
- Blue adapter: Use with sketch pens
- Gray adapter: Use with deep-cut blade, original-style premium blades
- White adapter: Use with 2mm kraft blade

Notes:

- A number on top of the blade (or the adapter, if needed) indicates which tool chamber to use.
- The numbers around the blade housing indicate blade depth.
- Different-colored tops distinguish the blades from each other.

TIP

When using the rotary blade, Silhouette Studio adds a series of hooks and loops to your design so that the blade can adjust its direction and continue cutting. Here's what the hooks and loops look like in the software.

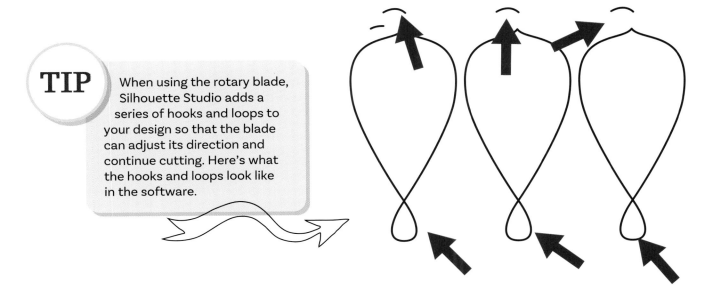

Using the Silhouette Cameo

The Cameo 4, Cameo 4 Plus, and Cameo 4 Pro are the current models in the Cameo family, but previous models are still supported by Silhouette America. All three models feature both cutting with a mat and matless cutting.

Silhouette Studio is a very powerful graphics software. While you can upgrade to unlock additional tools, we will look at some of its basic features. When you open the software, you'll see a blank workspace with a virtual mat in the center of the screen. The tools on the left allow you to select and create design elements. The tools on the right allow you to manipulate items in the workspace. The top toolbar is a dynamic toolbar, so the tools displayed will vary depending on the items selected in the workspace.

Access designs purchased from the Silhouette Store by clicking on the Library tab in the top left corner. Either double-click on the design or right-click and select Merge (design name) to place the design in the workspace. You can also open designs purchased from other sources, including designs stored on your computer, and you can combine design elements from multiple files.

Left-click on and drag the handles to size a design element: the corner handles adjust the height and width in proportion, and the top and side handles skew the design size. For more precise sizing, use the Scale tab in the Transform panel.

To add text, click on the Text tool in the left toolbar. Move your cursor into the workspace and left click to get a blinking cursor, then enter your text. Use the Text panel in the right toolbar to select the font, font size, text alignment, and more. Silhouette Studio uses all the fonts installed on your computer.

I like to fill my objects and text with color to get a good idea of what my design will look like when it is finished. There are separate tools for adding color to objects and to the cut lines around them. You can also use the Fill panel to add gradients and fill patterns to your designs.

Like many graphics programs, Silhouette Studio allows you to group items together so they

File Types

Vector files: These files are ready to cut and do not need to be traced. They are mathematically created and can be resized without degrading the image. This means that circles stay circles and smooth lines stay smooth. Common vector file types are SVG, AI, CDR, DXF, STUDIO (Silhouette cutters), and FCM (ScanNCut).

Raster files: These are image files and are not ready to cut. They need to be traced to create cut lines. When you trace them, the lines can be jagged, requiring some point editing to get clean cut lines. These images can become pixelated (distorted) when resized. Raster file types include JPG, PNG, BMP, and TIFF. These files work great for the print part of print-and-cut designs.

function as one for purposes of sizing, moving about the workspace, or aligning with other objects. Grouped items are unique in that they retain their individual characteristics and can be ungrouped and edited as needed.

When you are ready to cut your design, click on the Send tab in the top right corner of the workspace. You will get a preview window that shows you exactly what will be cut (or drawn if using drawing pens). You can set your material type and check the settings for your cut before loading your material on your mat and loading the mat into the Cameo. Before cutting your entire design, perform a test cut to check your settings. When your settings are correct, press Send, and that part of your design will be cut.

Silhouette Studio allows you to add "user-defined settings" for materials that are not in the included list of cut settings. For example, I created my own settings for rhinestones, so I don't have to do a lot of testing and fine-tuning when I am ready to cut rhinestone flock—I just select it as the material. Of course, I still do a test cut each time!

Brother ScanNCut

The Brother ScanNCut is available from a variety of sources, and where you buy your machine determines the features it includes. For example, the machines have a variety of built-in lettering styles and designs, and some also include Disney™ designs for personal use. All models come with a 12" x12" (30.5 x 30.50cm) mat, a blade holder, and a standard blade, and additional accessories come in certain bundles. Matless cutting is an option with some ScanNCut models with the addition of the roll feeder, which allows cuts up to 6' (1.8m). Newer ScanNCut models feature an autoblade that automatically senses the thickness of the material on the mat, so there is no need to adjust settings before cutting.

The ScanNCut's built-in scanner sets the machine apart from other cutters. You can scan your mat to see materials placed on the mat for accurate placement. You can also scan materials for immediate cutting (Direct Cut) or to use in your computer (Scan to Cut Data).

Another way in which the ScanNCut differs from the other brands we are discussing is that it does not need to communicate with a computer to cut or scan. All the controls are built into the machine and are accessed via the display on the machine.

To send designs to the machine, you can communicate either wirelessly or with a USB drive. Brother's free CanvasWorkspace software is available online or as a download. You can use this program to create or manipulate designs and then save them to a USB or send them wirelessly to your ScanNCut for cutting.

The ScanNCut uses FCM and SVG cut files. Saving a design in CanvasWorkspace creates a project file that cannot be cut but can be edited and then exported as an FCM file. The DX ScanNCut models also read PES, PHC, and PHX embroidery files so you can quickly and easily cut fabric for your appliqué embroidery projects.

Separate starter kits for rhinestones, foil transfer (glue), printable stickers, calligraphy, embossing, and paper piercing add functionality to the ScanNCut and CanvasWorkspace. The kits include all the tools and supplies necessary to get started with these techniques. Registering a starter kit unlocks its features in the ScanNCut and/or the software.

TIPS

• The ScanNCut DX automatically adjusts the depth of the blade by measuring an empty area at the top of the mat and then the area where your material is placed. Be sure not to put any material or tape in the top area, or your blade depth may not be set correctly.

• When cutting materials like vinyl or sticker paper (materials with a backing or carrier sheet) on a ScanNCut DX, be sure to turn on Half Cut in the settings so it will cut the material but not the backing or carrier sheet.

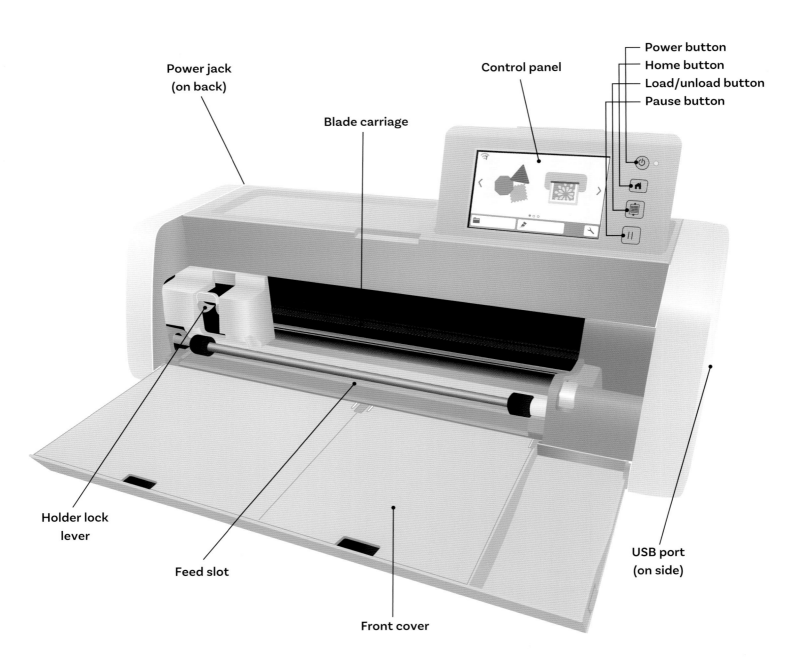

Power jack
(on back)

Blade carriage

Control panel

Power button
Home button
Load/unload button
Pause button

Holder lock
lever

Feed slot

USB port
(on side)

Front cover

Notes:
- The ScanNCut has only one tool chamber.
- The numbers around the blade housing indicate blade depth.
- Different colors distinguish the blades from each other.
- A rotary blade is now available for the ScanNCut.

ScanNCut Blades

Standard-cut blade holder and blade for CM and DC models

- Great for a wide variety of vinyl, paper, and fabric projects

Vinyl autoblade for DX models

- Requires the vinyl starter kit; cuts intricate vinyl patterns and tiny details

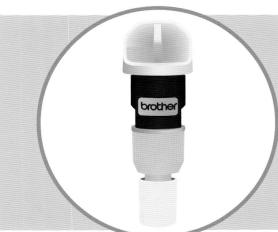

Deep-cut blade holder and blade for CM and DC models

- Designed for cutting thick materials such as felt, denim, and even leather

Thin fabric blade (not shown) for DX models

- Designed for cutting quilting and appliqué fabrics without fusible backing, ranging from 0.25 to 0.5mm in thickness

Using the Brother ScanNCut

As I mentioned, no software is required to operate the ScanNCut, and you can use Brother's free CanvasWorkspace software to create designs and utilize various starter kits that increase the software's capabilities.

When you turn on your ScanNCut, you will see a welcome screen and possibly a screen saver. Tap the screen to get to the main screen. From there, you can select the built-in patterns, start scanning a project (see Scanning with ScanNCut at right), or retrieve designs you have stored on the machine or on a USB drive.

Retrieve Data allows you to select the location of your design. You can retrieve data from your machine or a USB drive, you can send data wirelessly if your machine is Bluetooth-enabled, or you can plug your computer directly into the ScanNCut.

Use the arrows to scroll through the designs, then tap the one you want to use. You will get a preview of the design to make sure it is what you want to use. If you don't want to use the pictured design, just press the back button. Whatever you do, don't tap on the trash can icon, or you will delete the design. (Ask me how I know!)

Tapping OK will place the design. On the next screen, you can tap Add to add another design to be cut. You can also either edit the design currently on the screen or tap OK to move on.

When you tap Edit, you will see your item(s). If you have more than one item on the screen, you can toggle between them with the left/right arrows in the Select area. If you no longer want the selected design, tap the trash can—in this case, it will only be deleted from the workspace, not deleted permanently.

Tapping Object Edit brings you to another edit screen. Among the functions located here are Scale, Rotate, Duplicate, Add a Border, Flip, Align, and

Scanning with ScanNCut

In addition to being able to scan the mat to check the location of materials on your mat, there are two other scanning modes: Direct Cut and Scan to Cut Data. You can also scan to a USB drive.

Using Direct Cut allows you to scan the image on your mat and cut the image. This is great for cutting around images you have printed using your printer, like gift tags, planner stickers, and more. Using this technique, the cut information is not saved after scanning.

Using Scan to Cut Data allows you to scan an image and save it to use with your CanvasWorkspace software. Once scanned, the design will be saved, and you can access it by selecting Retrieve Data from the main screen or by sending it to your computer and manipulating it there.

Weld. Tapping one of these opens a new dialog box specific to that function so you can make your edits.

When you've finished editing and exited the Object Edit screen, you will be prompted to select what you want to do next: Cut, Draw, Emboss, or Foil. At this point, you are almost ready to cut! You have the option of turning on Half Cut as well as adding a test cut.

You have one more chance to check your settings before you cut. By tapping the Scan Mat icon, you can scan your mat to see the materials on your mat and check the placement of your designs. Finish by tapping Start and then cutting your design.

Cricut

Models in the Cricut Explore Series and the Cricut Maker are currently available in a variety of colors. These models have a 12" (30.5cm) cutting width and will cut up to 2 feet (61cm) in length. You can take advantage of the dual carriage to use two tools at once. Bluetooth compatibility lets you send designs to your digital cutter wirelessly. The Maker has a built-in USB port for charging a mobile device and a docking slot that makes it easy to send designs from your mobile device.

In addition to the cutting, drawing, and scoring tools that come with Explore models, the Maker comes with a rotary blade, a knife blade, and tools for embossing, engraving, and more. Many Cricut Maker blades and tools work with QuickSwap™ technology, which allows you to use one blade housing and change just the tips to use a variety of tools.

Cricut's Design Space software is available for both computers and mobile devices, and it includes ready-to-create projects and designs as well as tools for creating and editing your own designs. You can purchase fonts and designs individually or join Cricut Access for unlimited access to designs and fonts. When you have finished designing, you just click Make It, and Design Space separates all the colors into individual mats for easy cutting.

Design Space will open SVG files. It will also import JPG, PNG, GIF, and BMP image files for tracing.

Using the Cricut

Cricut Design Space resides on your computer, and you will need Internet access to utilize many of its features. When you launch the software, the home page will show you all your saved projects as well as projects available for purchase and download.

To get started on a new design, click on the New Project icon. The design workspace is called the canvas, and here are its main features:

- The tools down the left side allow you to create objects and bring images into the workspace.
- The dynamic toolbar at the top of the screen will change to display tools that are appropriate for the element selected.
- On the right side of the screen is the layers panel, where you can select different parts of a design to edit.

To browse a wide variety of backgrounds for your design, click on the Templates icon in the left toolbar. Once you select a template and it is placed on your workspace, click on the Images icon to select designs to add to your project. There are filters you can use to help narrow your search, and you can search for files by name.

To see the free designs available to you, click on the "+" by the Ownership filter and select Free. All the free designs will be displayed in the preview window. To select a design and place it in your workspace, click on it and then click Insert Image. You can change the size of the design by left-clicking and dragging the corner handle of the bounding box or by entering a value in the dynamic toolbar.

To add text, click on the Text icon in the left toolbar. When the text box appears, you can enter your text. Left-click and drag the text box wherever you want to place it on your design. With the text selected, click on the Font dropdown and choose a font you like from the fonts installed on your computer. To add text to more than one area of your design, create multiple text boxes and

TIP Design Space's Print Then Cut feature enables you to do just what it suggests: print a design and then cut quickly and easily around it.

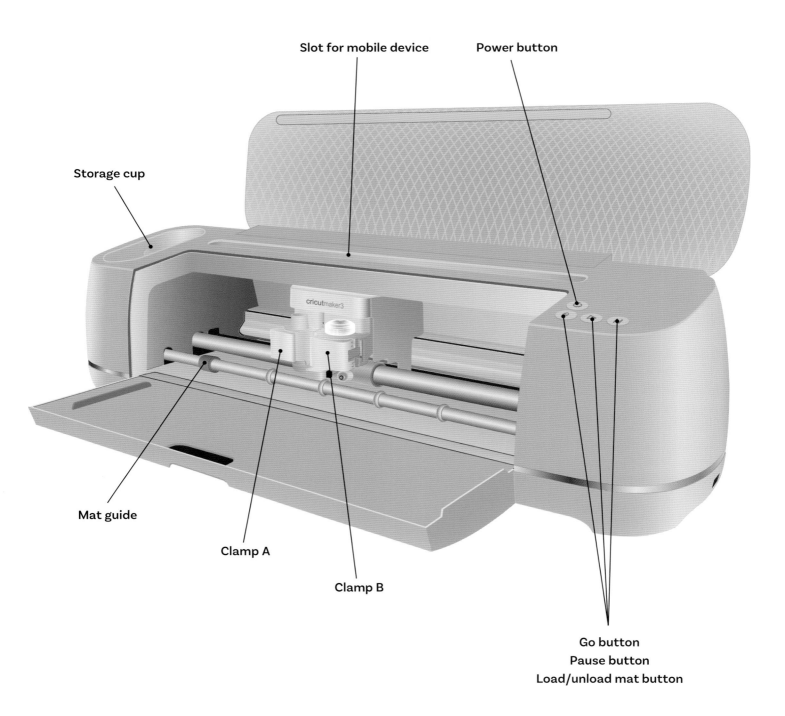

Slot for mobile device

Power button

Storage cup

Mat guide

Clamp A

Clamp B

Go button
Pause button
Load/unload mat button

Test Cutting with Design Space

Design Space does not have an automatic test cut, but you can create your own by adding a small shape to your design. Make it a color that is not already in your design and move it to the top of the list when you get to the Make window. A test cut will help you determine if you've selected the correct cut settings before sending your design to cut. The software settings are designed for "a perfect world" and do not take the age of your blade or the brand of material into consideration. Using a test cut will allow you to check your settings before sending your entire design to cut and then finding out the settings needed to be adjusted.

Cricut Design Space app

arrange them the way you want. If you select all text boxes in the Layers panel, then select Group, you will then be able to manipulate them as a group.

Send a design to cut by clicking on Make It in the top right corner. You will then see the Prepare window, which shows you the different parts of your design. Here, you can mirror the design if needed (e.g., if you are cutting HTV).

To cut, click Continue. In the Make window, you will be prompted to plug in your Cricut machine if it is not already plugged in. Select your material and check your settings: make sure you have the correct blade and your material is loaded on the mat correctly. If cutting another material, after the first material cuts, remove the mat and place your second material on the mat. Check your settings and make your second cut.

Cricut Blades and Tools

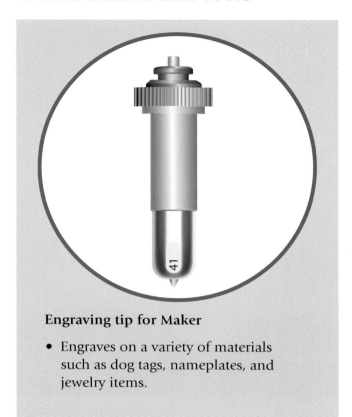

Engraving tip for Maker

- Engraves on a variety of materials such as dog tags, nameplates, and jewelry items.

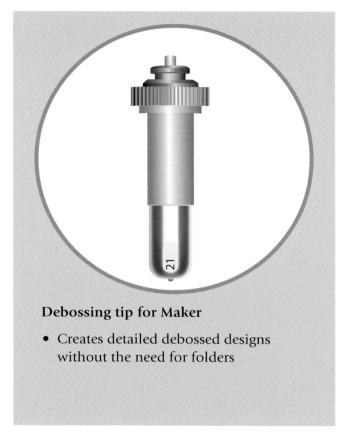

Debossing tip for Maker

- Creates detailed debossed designs without the need for folders

Scoring wheels for Maker

- Fine scoring wheel works with thinner materials

- Deep scoring wheel makes extra-deep score lines on thicker materials

Wavy blade for Maker

- Creates wavy cut lines

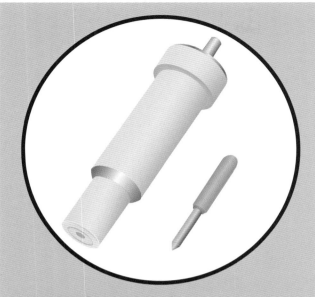

Bonded-fabric blade

- Cuts bonded fabric or fabric with fusible backing
- Pink blade and housing to match the fabric-grip mat

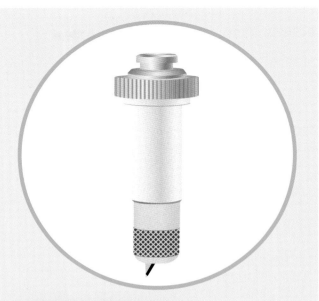

Knife blade for Maker

- Cuts thicker or denser materials such as leather, craft foam, and balsa wood; adds dimension and texture

Rotary blade for Maker

- Cuts thinner materials and fabrics without backing

Scoring stylus (not shown)

- Creates score lines for folding cardstock to create 3D projects, cards, boxes, envelopes, and more

Notes:

- The number near the bottom of each blade is the item number.
- Cricut Maker's Tool Slot A has a preinstalled adapter for pens; all other quick-change blades use Tool Slot B.

Mats

Silhouette Cameo Mats

- **Standard-tack mat:** This mat is included with Cameo models. It has a standard adhesive level and is suitable for most materials.

- **Light-tack mat:** The light-tack mat has a lighter adhesive level and is designed to hold thinner materials like copy paper, vellum, and similar specialty materials.

- **Strong-tack mat:** Designed to hold thicker materials and fabric, this mat has the strongest adhesive level.

- **PixScan mat:** The PixScan Mat allows you to cut precisely around an object in a specific location on the mat. Used with your camera or scanner, this mat works great for "fussy cutting."

Cameo light-tack mat

Cricut light-grip mat

ScanNCut Mats

Note: There are different mats for the different ScanNCut models.

- **Standard cutting mat:** Used with fabric, vinyl, and paper.

- **Low-tack adhesive mat:** Used with delicate or thin paper.

- **Scanning mat:** Used for scanning photos and artwork. ScanNCut will not cut materials placed on this mat.

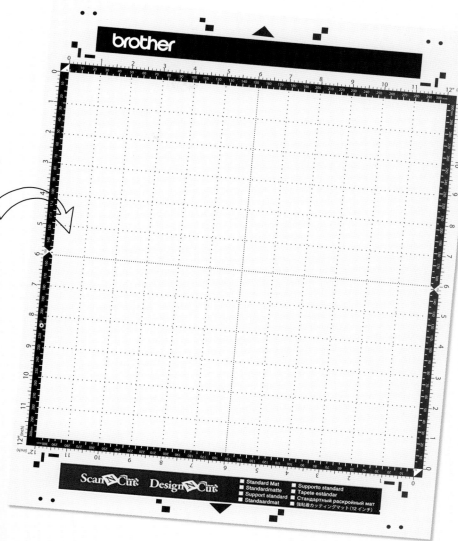

ScanNCut standard cutting mat

Cricut Mats

- **Standard cutting mat:** Included with most Cricut cutters, it holds most materials well. It is available in 12" x 12" (30.5 x 30.5cm) and 12" x 24" (30.5 x 61cm) sizes.

- **Light-grip mat:** This mat offers a lighter grip, designed for use with vellum, paper, and cardstock.

- **Strong-grip mat:** Used with thicker materials like textured cardstock, fabric with backing material, and matboard.

- **Fabric-grip mat:** Used with thinner materials and fabrics without backing. It is designed specifically for use with the bonded-fabric blade and the rotary blade, and it is pink to match the bonded-fabric blade.

Common Materials for Digital Cutting

Your digital cutting machine will cut a wide variety of materials quickly and easily. The step-by-step projects featured in this book are for the sewist, the quilter, the lover of soft goods. Whether using vinyl to make a sign to display your passion, cotton for a unique baby gift, felt to whip up some easy holiday ornaments, or leather for a make-today-wear-tonight set of earrings, the collection of projects in the Digital Cutting Inspiration gallery (see page 8) encourages you to try out a variety of materials to see how versatile your digital cutting machine can be.

Adhesive Vinyl

Adhesive vinyl is designed to be placed on hard surfaces. Adhesive vinyl comes in a variety of colors, thicknesses, and recommended usages. Because of these differences, each vinyl may have different cut settings, so always do a test cut before cutting your project. The "Create" wall hanging, phone case, and hexagon collage projects shown in the Digital Cutting Inspiration gallery (see page 8) use adhesive vinyl. The following chart shows some different types of adhesive vinyl products.

PRODUCT EXAMPLES	DESCRIPTION
Oracal® 631 Siser® Easy PSV™	Matte-finish vinyl; removable for up to two years. Considered wall-safe because it does not damage walls when removed.
Oracal 641	Matte-finish vinyl; estimated three- to five-year life. Great for both indoor and outdoor applications.
Oracal 651 StyleTech 4000	Glossy finish; estimated five- to eight-year life. One of the most commonly used adhesive vinyl types. Popular for cups, signs, and other indoor projects as well as outdoor projects.
Oracal 8300	Transparent and UV-stable; perfect for stained-glass projects. Can be layered to create a wide variety of colors and effects.

Heat Transfer Vinyl

Heat transfer vinyl (HTV) is usually applied to fabric, other soft surfaces, and wood. When applying it to fabric, you must negate the effect of seams, straps, or other thick areas for proper adhesion because the press will not make even contact with the vinyl. Poor pressure can cause the vinyl to lift even before washing! (See the Press Pillows section on page 54.) The gift bags (page 90), "Dream" wall hanging (page 11), and mitten ornament (page 82) all make use of HTV.

PRODUCT TYPES	DESCRIPTION
Smooth HTV	Siser® EasyWeed® is often considered the industry standard; ThermoFlex Plus is another popular brand. Thinner than many other brands of HTV. Can be layered; can be peeled hot or cold.
Smooth HTV (Thin)	EasyWeed Stretch is thin and stretchy, making it great for performance apparel, T-shirts, baby garments, and more. Can be layered; can be peeled hot or cold. ThermoFlex Stretch is a similar product, but it cannot be layered.
Smooth HTV (Thick)	Siser Brick® 600 HTV is an example of a product that is thicker than standard smooth HTV. It has a matte finish and is used to add texture and dimension. Layerable as a base layer for an embossed look. Cold peel.
Glitter HTV	Brings sparkle to your project; complements rhinestones and smooth HTV. Can be layered on top of smooth HTV. Do not layer on top of glitter. Because of its texture, you cannot get even pressure for anything layered on top, which can cause lifting. Warm peel.
Holographic HTV	Color-changing chips add depth, dimension, and sparkle; use alone or in place of rhinestones. Do not layer anything on top. Cold peel.
Adhesive HTV	Use alone for tone-on-tone look. Often pressed onto a garment with foil applied on top and heated to add a budget-friendly shiny look. Can be layered; hot peel.
Printed HTV	Adds pattern and color to projects. Does not have carrier sheet because ink is applied on top of vinyl. No need to mirror designs—designs go on mat with pretty side up! After cutting, apply heat-resistant mask over printed HTV, remove backing sheet, and press to project.
Foil HTV	Quick and easy addition to projects. "Dream" sign (page 11) uses heat-reactive foil.

Note: Smooth (all varieties), glitter, holographic, and adhesive HTV have a shiny carrier sheet attached. Mirror the design before cutting, then place the HTV on the mat with the shiny carrier sheet on the vinyl. Once weeded, the carrier sheet provides a covering for the HTV to protect it from direct contact with the heat press.

Holographic
HTV

Pressing HTV

Getting your HTV to adhere well and wash well requires the right combination of time, temperature, and pressure. Using a heat press is the most effective way to press HTV onto your garments because you can accurately set all three of these variables. Plus, the pressure is applied by the press, not by you.

If you do not have a heat press, you can use a home iron with the following important advice in mind:

- It's preferable to use an iron with no steam holes in the soleplate, as the holes can cause spots of uneven pressure.
- Do not use steam when applying HTV with a home iron.
- Press by applying the iron for the prescribed amount of time, then lifting it and moving it to the next location, if needed. *Do not "iron" by moving your iron around on the vinyl.* Press, lift, repeat.
- Do not press on your ironing board; ironing boards can be a little squishy. Iron on a hard surface with no cushion or give. Press on a tile or use a specially designed heat-press pad to protect your countertop or table.

Foil HTV Tips

- Using a cover sheet causes foil to appear less shiny.
- Foil picks up texture. Use parchment paper instead of Teflon when pressing; Teflon will leave texture marks in your foil.
- Gently rub to remove any flaking.
- If foil gets a rainbow or wavy look, your temperature is too high.
- If foil looks crinkly after pressing, use more pressure when pressing.

More HTV Tips

- Check the manufacturer's instructions for your HTV. Different brands have different time and temperature settings, so always check before pressing. Pressing too long can cause the adhesive to break down, and the HTV will not adhere well to your project.
- Also pay attention to the recommendations for hot, warm, or cold peel. Peeling too soon can cause the vinyl to separate or lift, and your project will be ruined.
- Cut HTV shiny side down. If it's hard to tell which side is the shiny side, run your fingertips over the HTV; the shiny side will feel smoother.
- Remember to mirror (or flip horizontally) your design if you're using HTV.
- Patterned iron-on vinyl is very similar to regular vinyl, but it will need heat-resistant transfer tape. You do not need to mirror printed HTV.

Fabric

I love using fabric in my digital cutters, and success with fabric requires just a little preparation. Digital cutting machines are an absolute dream for cutting appliqués, fabric flower petals, shapes for quilting, felt ornaments, and more. Here are my best tips for working with fabric:

- You can use any standard or autoblade to cut fabric. No special blade is needed for stabilized fabric.
- A rotary blade is designed to allow you to cut fabric without stabilizing the fabric.

- Use lightweight fusible interfacing to provide stability when cutting fabric for sewing or embroidery. I like Heat n Bond Lite because it will not gum up your needle. Be sure to follow the manufacturer's instructions when using a fusible product—not all products are applied in the same way!
- No-sew fusible interfacing is heavier and is used for products that do not involve sewing. These products will gum up your needle if used in sewing projects—and a needle gummed up with adhesive will cause your thread to break. Again, follow the manufacturer's instructions. Overheating can cause the product not to adhere properly.
- Terial Magic is my favorite spray-on stabilizer; it makes your fabric paper-stiff. Made using an organic natural compound, Terial Magic is safe to use on most natural fabrics. It won't leave residue on your iron or gum up your needles, and it washes out completely.

How to Use Terial Magic

1. Spray your fabric to saturate it with Terial Magic. Alternatively, pour Terial Magic into a bowl or plastic bag and add the fabric. Saturate the fabric.
2. Check for dry spots and respray or soak as needed.
3. Hang to dry for ten to fifteen minutes.
4. Press (do not iron!) the fabric. Moving the iron across the fabric can stretch and distort the fabric. Press, lift, reposition, repeat.
5. Press until the fabric is dry and stiff, like paper.
6. If desired, you can add fusible interfacing for additional stability.

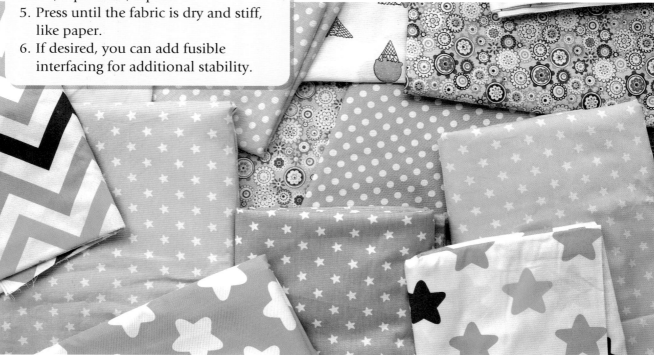

Felt

No prep is needed for felt when using rotary blades. Use a strong-tack mat and make sure the felt is completely and securely adhered to the mat so it does not move. Felt can be cut with a rotary blade. Designs should not be overly intricate or complex when using the rotary blades on felt.

Leatherette and Ultrasuede

Lightweight leather and Ultrasuede® materials are handled in the same manner and can be cut on most cutters. Not all textured leatherette products cut well due to the uneven surface, and some faux-suede products can fray. I have had great success with leatherette from Silhouette America. The patterned and textured leathers shown here are from The Leather Guy®, and the suede is from Sensuede®. Every material will be different, so make test cuts to check your settings before sending your cut job or investing in a lot of yardage. Because these are thicker materials, use simpler designs—overly intricate designs or small designs with lot of details do not cut well. You can add more detail if the overall design is larger.

- Use a strong-tack mat to help hold these thicker materials in place. I have also used painter's tape to hold these materials in place for cutting.
- For an added custom touch, consider adding detail to your leatherette with HTV. I also put HTV on the back of certain leatherette projects, such as earrings, to "finish" the back.
- After cutting, press rhinestones onto your leatherette for added bling! Just be careful that you don't leave impressions of the iron on the material. If your rhinestone design (and transfer tape) does not cover the entire design, use parchment paper on top of the leatherette to protect it from the press or iron.
- Some leatherette will accept alcohol inks. Use sponge applicators to apply ink. While the ink is wet, you can blow on the ink to move it around on the leatherette. Applying a spritz of rubbing alcohol will add extra texture and dimension to your ink, further customizing your design.
- If adding vinyl details to leather, use parchment paper between your iron and the leather to prevent any damage to your materials.

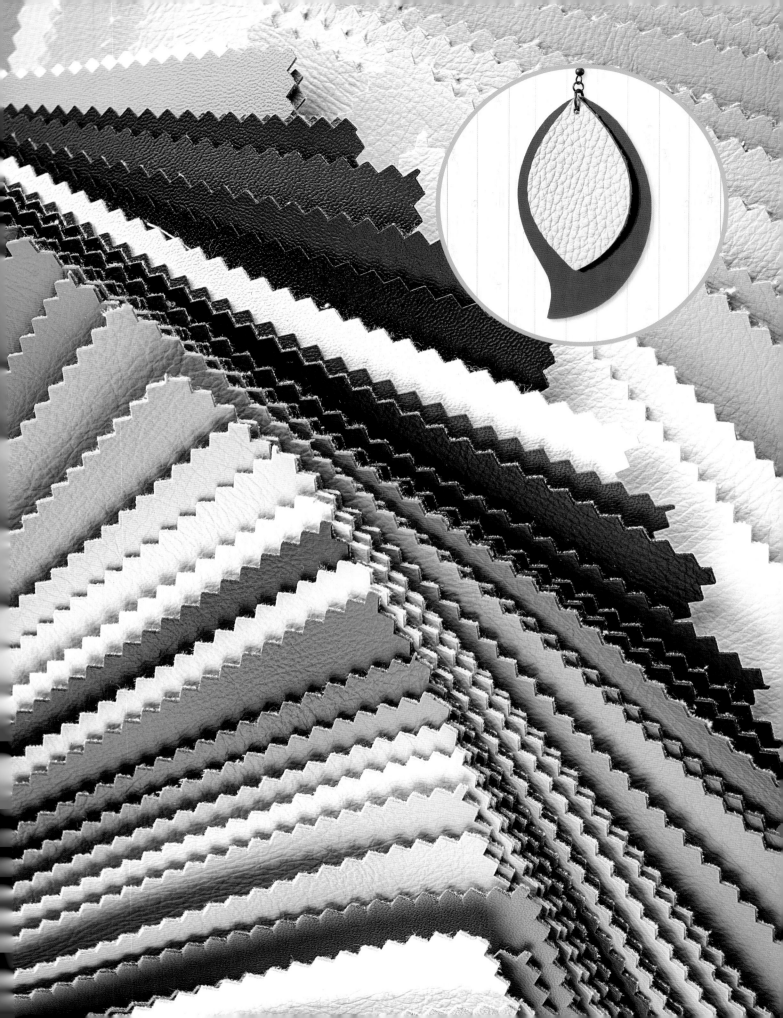

Techniques to Know

I know you are anxious to get to the projects, but please take a few moments to explore the techniques in this section. Included are step-by-step instructions and tips for common techniques like weeding and working with transfer tape, using special products like glitter laminate and etching cream, and working with rhinestones.

Weeding

Weeding is the process of removing any unwanted material from your cut designs so that the image you intend to transfer to your project is clean, with no background vinyl. When the vinyl comes out of the digital cutting machine, it is still a sheet or square with the cut lines defining the design. Use a weeding tool to pull away the background (or negative) vinyl around the design lines before applying transfer tape. Weeding on your mat can help hold your project steady, but you do not need to leave your project on the mat to weed. However, a lightbox or an illuminated pad made specifically for crafters is useful with more intricate projects to ensure you don't weed out part of the design.

For reverse weeding, apply the transfer tape to the vinyl after it is cut and removed from the machine. Use your squeegee tool on front and back to make sure the tape is secure, then remove the transfer tape backing to weed from the wrong side of your designs.

1. A digital-cut design before weeding.

2. The negative material is pulled away from the cut design.

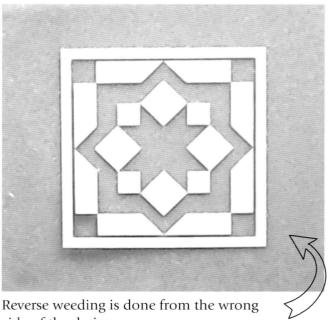

3. After weeding, the design is ready to be transferred to the project.

Reverse weeding is done from the wrong side of the design.

Using Transfer Tape

Use transfer tape to remove the cut pieces from the vinyl backing and "transfer" them to your project's surface after weeding. Place a sheet of transfer tape, sticky side down and covering your design, and use your squeegee tool to make sure all the cut pieces are secure. Then peel up the design and position it on your project. For larger projects with multiple pieces, you can transfer piece by piece. Some transfer tapes have grid lines for easy alignment.

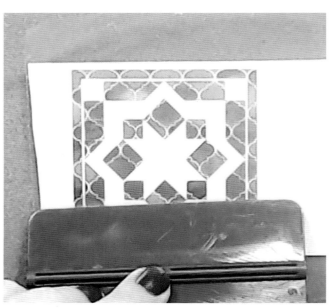

1. Transfer a design by first covering it with transfer tape, sticky side down.

2. Use the squeegee tool to ensure full contact between the transfer tape and all design pieces.

Adding a Laminate Overlay

Working with patterned adhesive vinyl is the same as working with solid-colored adhesive vinyl when it comes to cutting, but in the case of the printed vinyl, you need to consider the end use of the finished project. If the item is something that will be handled or touched, like the Quilt-Lover's Phone Case (see page 10), I always take the extra step of adding a laminate overlay to the vinyl before cutting. Over time, the oils on your hands will cause the printed vinyl to fade and become less vibrant, and adding an overlay will keep this from happening.

Applying a laminate is easy. If the design is small, you can just remove the backing from the laminate and apply it to your vinyl. If the design is larger, try the hinge method on the opposite page. This method works great for getting the laminate on your vinyl with few (or no) bubbles.

After you've applied the laminate, you are ready to cut your design. Remember that this vinyl is thicker than normal with the laminate added, so you will need to adjust your cut settings. I usually start with a cardstock setting when cutting vinyl with a laminate overlay. Be sure to perform a test cut and make adjustments as needed before cutting the design. The design file for this project is Phone Case.svg.

The Hinge Method

1. Cut a piece of printed vinyl large enough for your design.

2. Cut a piece of laminate the same size as your vinyl.

3. Place the printed vinyl on your work surface with the print side looking at you.

4. Lay the laminate over the vinyl and check the size.

5. Take a piece of painter's tape or other tape and place it across the middle of the laminate.

6. Pull the laminate back at one end so you can see the backing. Gently remove the laminate from the backing, stopping at the tape.

7. Cut the backing away from the laminate.

8. Using a squeegee, *slowly* work the exposed laminate back over the printed vinyl. Don't hurry, because you might cause bubbles in the laminate.

9. Remove the backing from the remaining laminate and smooth it into position on the printed vinyl.

10. Remove the tape when you have finished.

Note: Don't worry if you get a few bubbles when you apply the laminate. They will usually disappear after a few days as the vinyl cures. If they do not, pop the bubbles with a small sharp object, like a pin or your weeding tool, and gently press the laminate down onto the vinyl.

Using Etching Cream on Glass and Slate

Etching cream is used with a stencil to create permanent designs on glass, mirrors, slate, or metal. The etching cream essentially "eats" a design into the material's surface.

When selecting a motif to use with etching cream, choose a design that will work well as a stencil. Designs with a lot of detail and/or small pieces will require extra care when cutting and transferring the stencil to the item you are etching.

Start by cleaning the surface of your project with an alcohol wipe to remove any oils or other debris. Apply the stencil to your chosen surface using transfer tape, then weed. When applying the stencil, the key is to carefully position it and press it down around all the edges so your etching cream cannot seep underneath the stencil. This is especially crucial if you are working on a textured surface, such as slate.

Once you've secured the stencil and removed the transfer tape, spread and apply the etching cream with a foam brush. Be sure to dab; if you rub or brush (even gently), you risk moving small pieces or lifting edges. Read the manufacturer's instructions to determine how long you should leave the etching cream on the surface; leaving it on for longer than the recommended time does not usually produce better results.

The final step is to rinse away any excess etching cream and remove the stencil. It may not look like the etching has taken effect when it is still wet, but it will be much more pronounced and visible when dry.

TIP Avoid applying text that wraps around the jar, because it will be difficult to read. Use painter's tape to create a guideline for your word placement.

Etching a Button Jar

1. Gather your materials. You'll need glass etching cream, a glass jar of your choice, a paintbrush, painter's tape, a microfiber cloth, permanent or stencil vinyl, rubber gloves, and your digital cutting tools. You'll also need the design file Buttons.svg.

2. Clean the surface of the jar with warm, soapy water and dry with a microfiber cloth. Be sure to remove all fingerprints or dirt from the surface you plan to etch.

3. Create the stencil. Using your digital cutter's software, upload the button design and create an inverted image of the template as follows: Place a rectangle over the word "Buttons" until the words are completely covered. Select both the rectangle and the words. (If using Cricut Design Space, then select Slice.) From there, delete all extra pieces so that your stencil looks like the image below.

4. Weed, then place the stencil on the jar. Make sure there are no gaps or pulls in the vinyl as you place it down. Remove the transfer tape. Check—and double-check and triple-check—for any gaps and firmly press all over the vinyl. This is very important because you do not want the etching cream to get under your stencil. Once the stencil is in place, use more painter's tape to create an additional barrier around the stencil.

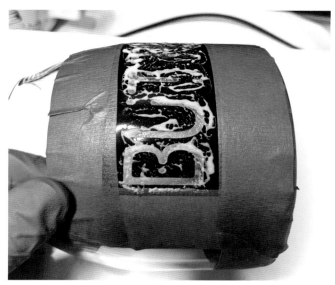

5. Before applying the etching cream, stir it well. Then, using your foam brush, apply the etching cream to the lettering as smoothly as possible. It's important that you have enough product on the brush before the first dab on the glass. If it is too dry, the etching will have an uneven, swiped appearance. After you've applied the initial layer, use your foam brush to move the etching cream around slightly in every direction so that you don't miss any corners or small spots.

6. Put on your rubber gloves and carefully rinse the glass jar in a sink. Do not allow the etching cream to touch any surface that you don't want etched. (This is why we added extra painter's tape.) Rub a gloved finger over the etched surface and rinse until the etching cream is completely washed away. Remove the tape and stencil. If some of the stencil remains on the glass surface, use the weeding tool to remove the pieces.

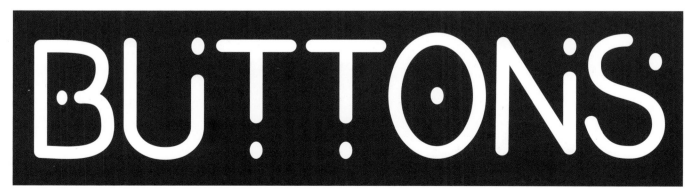

Stencil

Using Rhinestones and Rhinestone Flock

Rhinestones add that touch of bling that makes any creation special! I love creating with rhinestones and experimenting with different types. When it comes to rhinestones, the different digital cutter brands have very specific settings and approaches, which I've outlined here, and the rhinestone features are often upgrades that are not included with the machine. You'll also want some tools and materials that make working with rhinestones easier and much more fun.

Selecting Stones

Clarity is one of the most important considerations when purchasing rhinestones. You do not want stones that appear cloudy, as they will not have the shine and sparkle you want to add to your project. Remember that quality and price go hand in hand. If you skimp on the price, you are also skimping on the quality. In addition to not looking as nice, inexpensive stones may have inconsistent adhesive quality, meaning that they may not adhere well to your project.

The design file for the rhinestone design pictured is Rhinestone Butterflies.svg.

Types of Stones

Korean low-lead hot-fix rhinestones are widely used by retail manufacturers and crafters alike. Their high quality and bright shine are available at affordable prices, making them a suitable choice for almost all your projects. This type of rhinestone is available in the widest variety of sizes and colors.

Diamond-cut rhinestones have pointed facets that give them amazing sparkle. They are also priced affordably and popular with both retail manufacturers and crafters. They are slightly larger than Korean low-lead stones, so you will have to increase your stone size when cutting templates so the holes will be the right size.

Hot-fix rhinestones

Rhinestone Sizes

There are many different sizes of rhinestones. Rhinestone measurements are listed in "SS" sizes. The most commonly used sizes are:

SS6—2mm	SS16—4mm
SS10—3mm	SS20—5mm

Swarovski crystals are some of the most brilliant and beautiful stones available. They are more expensive than the other stones discussed, but they provide a sparkle like no other. I use these on special garments and projects.

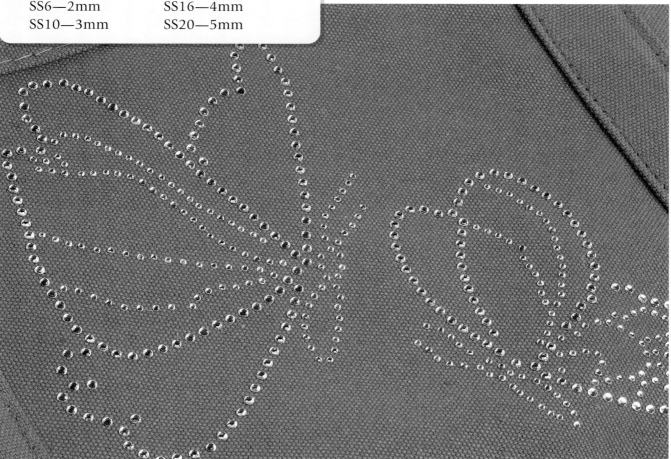

Tools for Working with Rhinestones

Rhinestone flock: Flock is the material on which you cut rhinestone templates. It comes on a roll. It is thicker than vinyl, has a suede-like feel, and has a sticky back with a paper backing. I like The Rhinestone World's Magic Flock.

Rhinestone brush: Use this soft-sided tool in a circular motion to brush your stones into the holes in your template. You can find these in the paint department of the hardware store. Use a lot of stones when adding stones to flock.

Tweezers: A good pair of tweezers will help you place and turn individual stones.

Rhinestone pick-up tool: This tool has sticky tips that make it perfect for picking up and placing small objects. The other end is usually tapered to assist in gently nudging stones into place.

Rhinestone scoop: The Rhinestone World makes a rhinestone scoop to help clean up stones quickly after your project is completed.

Brushing the stones into the template

Rhinestone flock

Filled flock

Ready to press

Rhinestone design on transfer tape

Rhinestone transfer tape: This heat-resistant two-part tape is used to pick the stones up from the flock template and transfer them to your project. Press your stones with this tape to protect the surface of the garment and the stones.

Using Purchased Designs

You can purchase designs from many sources, but purchased rhinestone designs cannot be resized. Let me repeat that: *purchased rhinestone designs cannot be resized!* Your software will see the design simply as a group of circles. If you attempt to resize them, each individual circle will be resized, and your stones will not fit in the holes properly. If you create the rhinestone design yourself with a rhinestone tool or module, you can resize the design as long as it is still in the software's native format.

TIP When applying transfer tape, do it with conviction! If you hesitate, static electricity will cause the stones to grab the transfer tape, and they will move out of position.

Setting Up Your Machine

Following are the recommended settings for cutting Magic Flock templates (not applicable to Cricut machines). Remember to always do a test cut.

Silhouette Cameo
- Blade depth: 6
- Speed: 10
- Force: 22
- Passes: 2

ScanNCut
- Cut speed: 3
- Cut pressure: 0
- Aqua blade: 6

TIP
- Press at 335°F for fifteen seconds (unless otherwise recommended by the manufacturer).
- Using a press pillow is recommended.
- If creating a multi-decoration (multi-dec) design, press the vinyl first, for just a few seconds, then press the stones.

Press Pillows

Digital cutting enthusiasts love to add HTV and/or rhinestones to their projects but find that seams, straps, and other bulky areas can interfere with the proper adhesion of these products. To offset seams or bulky areas, I recommend using a press pillow. I just insert the pillow into the blank or the leg of pants that have a bulky seam and press as usual.

Press pillows or press pads are available from a variety of sources, but you can make your own using a standard sewing machine for much less! All you need are some Teflon press sheets and ½" (1.3cm) high-density foam. I can create several press pillows from a package of five Teflon press sheets sized 16" x 20" (40.6 x 50.8cm). For the foam, I recommend 24" (61cm)–wide, ½" (1.3cm)–thick high-density foam, available by the yard.

Once you have gathered your supplies, decide what size pillows you want to create. The following sizes provide press pillows for a variety of projects. I made these pillows by cutting the Teflon sheets to size, and I had enough left over to make a variety of extra square and rectangular press pillows.
- 16" x 16" (40.6 x 40.6cm) press pillow for large pillow covers and tote bags
- 6.5" x 16" (16.5 x 40.6cm) press pillow for pant legs and sleeves
- 8" x 8" (20.3 x 20.3cm) and 5" x 5" (12.7 x 12.7cm) press pillows
- 11" x 11" (27.9 x 27.9cm) pillow for use with shirts

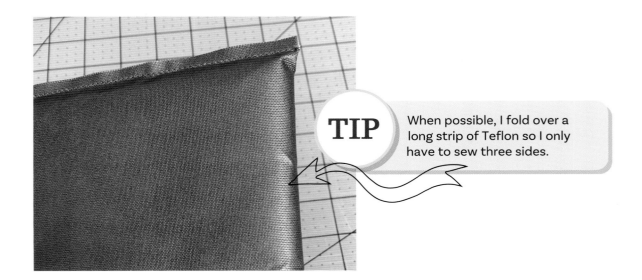

TIP
When possible, I fold over a long strip of Teflon so I only have to sew three sides.

Making a Press Pillow

MATERIALS AND TOOLS

- 6" x 12" (15.2 x 30.5cm) rectangle Teflon sheeting
- 5.25" x 5.25" square high-density foam (½" [1.3cm] thick)
- 30 wt. heavy-duty cotton thread
- Universal sewing machine needle
- Clover Wonder Clips®

Instructions

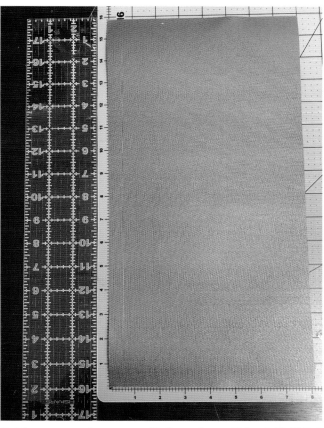

1. Measure and cut your Teflon sheet (8" x 16" [20.3 x 40.6cm] shown here for an 8" x 8" [20.3 x 20.3cm] pillow).

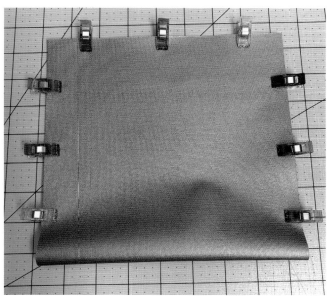

2. Fold the Teflon in half lengthwise. Clip with Wonder Clips to hold the edges together (Teflon sheets are slippery).

TIP

Trim your foam rectangle ¾" (1.9cm) smaller than the width of the pillow and ½" (1.3cm) smaller than the length of the pillow to account for the seam allowance and thickness of the foam if stitching only three sides. If you are stitching all four sides and not taking advantage of a folded side, the foam will need to be ¾" (1.9cm) smaller than your Teflon rectangle all around.

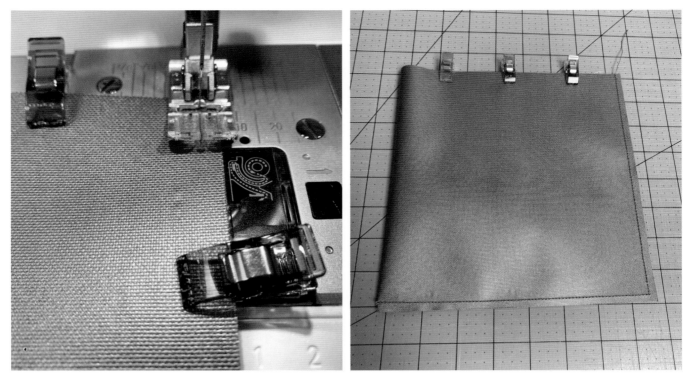

3. On your sewing machine, select a straight stitch and increase the stitch length to 4.0 to accommodate the thicker thread. Straight-stitch two open edges using a ¼" (0.6cm) allowance, removing the clips as you approach them. Backstitch to secure your stitching when you start and stop.

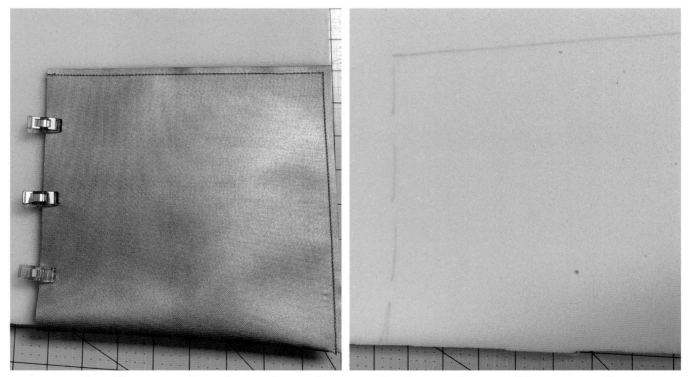

4. Remove the pillow cover from the machine. Place it on the foam and trace a filler piece smaller than the outer pillow to accommodate seam allowances and density. Cut out the foam piece and trim to fit as needed (see sidebar on page 55).

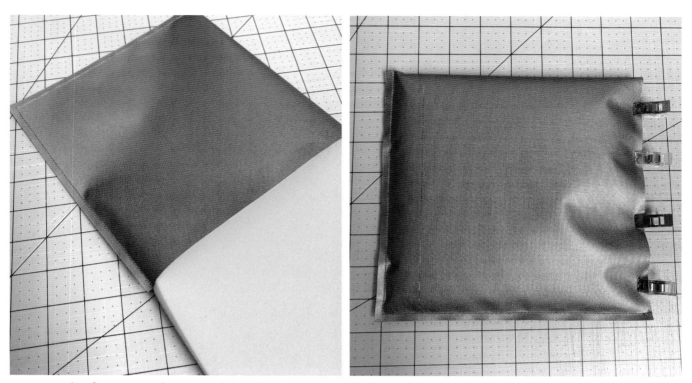

5. Insert the foam into the open side of the pillow cover and clip the opening closed.

6. Stitch the open side closed using a ¼" (0.6cm) seam; backstitch.

STEP-BY-STEP
PROJECTS

Children's Fox Apron

Whether crafting or helping in the kitchen, kids will have fun keeping their clothes clean with this precious fox friend apron. You can even stuff the ears for a little dimension. Appliqué the eyes or use buttons. It's a quick-and-easy project that's destined to bring many smiles to the recipient.

MATERIALS AND TOOLS

- 1 fat quarter orange cotton fabric
- 1 fat quarter white cotton fabric
- ⅛ yard (11.4cm) black cotton fabric
- ⅛ yard (11.4cm) pink cotton fabric
- Approximately ½ yard (45.7cm) Heat n Bond double-sided fusible web
- Child's size apron
- Two black buttons for eyes (optional)
- Fabric-grip (or standard-grip) cutting mat
- Brayer tool (optional)
- Small ironing board or mat
- Iron
- 1–2 oz. batting
- Embroidery thread in black, white, and orange
- Water-soluble stabilizer (I used Solvy®)
- Lightweight tear-away stabilizer
- Fox apron design files (Fox Face.svg and Fox Tail.svg)

Prepare the Materials

1. Using your cutting-machine's software, upload the provided fox apron design files. Size your file to the appropriate size for your apron.

2. Iron your apron and decide how big you want the fox face to be on the front; it's up to you! In the example, the fox takes up a majority of the front above the pockets and has stuffed ears.

3. Iron your material so there are no wrinkles or creases. If your orange and white fabrics exceed 12" (30.5cm) square, cut them down to that size. Your pink and black sections will be much smaller, so cut those fabrics to a size just slightly larger than your design so that you'll use less adhesive backing.

4. Attach double-sided fusible webbing, according to the manufacturer's instructions for temperature settings, to the back of each fabric that you need to cut. Using an iron, press the fabric to the adhesive backing for fifteen to thirty seconds. The adhesive backing should not peel from the fabric, so press again if necessary.

5. Once you've bonded the fabric, load the cutting mat with the fabric, adhesive side down. Cut the fabric using the bonded-fabric setting.

Appliqué on the Apron

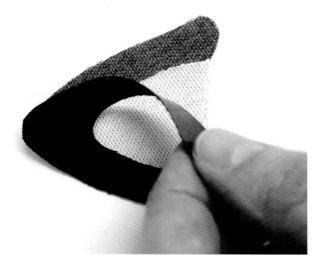

1. Peel the paper from the adhesive web on the back of the white inner ear piece. Center the white ear piece flush with the bottom edge of the orange ear piece and adhere with an iron. Repeat with the white piece for the second ear.

2. Remove the paper from the adhesive web of the black ear piece and layer it on top of one of the ear pieces with the edges flush. Press to adhere with an iron. Repeat with the black ear piece for the second ear.

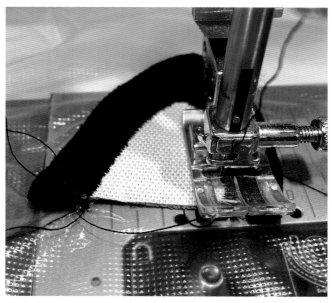

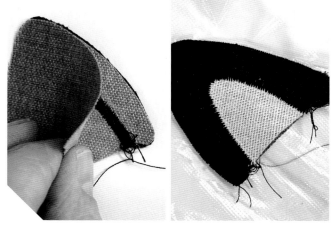

4. Match the appliquéd ear front with the orange ear back. Appliqué around the outer edge, joining the layers. Repeat for the second ear.

3. Take one of the layered ears to the machine, set for a satin stitch (length: 0.8, width: 3.0). Place the ear on a piece of stabilizer. Using black thread, appliqué around the inner ear. Repeat for the second ear.

TIP

When appliquéing dark thread on the edges of a project, a clear stabilizer like Solvy is a better choice than a white tear-away stabilizer, which can leave little crumbs of white paper behind.

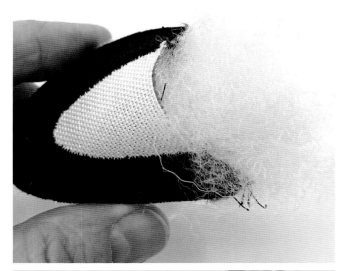

5. Stuff each ear with a little bit of batting, pushing the batting up into the point. Stitch across the bottom to secure.

6. Audition the fox face on top of the apron to determine where you want to position the ears. Pin the ears in place and take the apron to the machine. Remove the pins and stitch the ears in place on the apron front. Set aside.

7. Remove the paper backing from the fox face details, except for the nose piece, and apply to the head. Use the finished face photo as a placement guide.

8. Back the layered head piece with lightweight tear-away stabilizer and satin stitch around all the elements. Use a narrow zigzag (width: 2.0) around the eyes and cheeks, and a wider zigzag (width: 3.0) around the orange "fur."

9. Position and apply the tail to the apron, pressing with an iron. Use the finished apron photo for placement.

10. Remove the backing from the appliquéd head piece, position it on the apron front, and press with an iron. Press securely with the tip of the iron around the ear area.

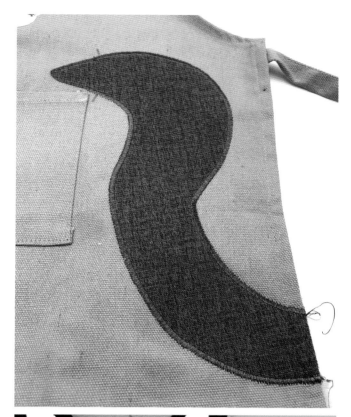

11. Back your stitching area with tear-away stabilizer, then appliqué around the face to secure it to the apron.

12. Remove the backing from the black nose piece, position and adhere it with an iron, then secure it with a satin stitch (width 3.0).

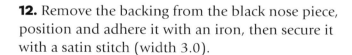

13. Mark where to start and stop zigzag stitching the tail so that it will continue partially under the white tip, then appliqué around the tail. Apply the white tail-tip piece and appliqué around it to complete the tail.

Raw-Edge Appliqué Owl Quilt

These adorable patchwork owls let you have so much fun with a layer cake, mixing and matching and raw-edge stitching to make a little quilt any baby boy or girl will love. You can choose to make the owls so that over time the edges of the owls will slightly fray, which is often a design approach of raw-edge appliqué. To do so, prepare the fabrics with Terial Magic before cutting, then cut and apply Heat n Bond to your individual owl pieces. Or, you can apply fusible web to your layer-cake squares before cutting, which will then secure all the edges of the owl pieces to the background square.

MATERIALS AND TOOLS

Finished size 34" x 43" (86.4cm x 1.1m)

Note: The following materials are used to create six owls.

- One layer-cake fabric bundle for owls and blocks (I used Lella Boutique Folktale)
- 1½ yards (1.4m) fabric for narrow border and backing (Lella Boutique Folktale Golden Gypsy)
- ⅓ yard (30.5cm) fabric for wide border (Lella Boutique Folktale Skinny Stripes Olive Green)
- ½ yard (45.7cm) fabric for binding (Lella Boutique Folktale Golden Magic Dot)
- Approximately 1 yard of Wonder-Under® interfacing (or Heat n Bond double-sided fusible web)
- 12" x 12" (30.5 x 30.5cm) fabric-grip (or standard-grip) cutting mat
- Brayer tool (optional)
- Small ironing board or mat
- Iron
- Silver-green thread for raw-edge stitching and quilting
- Coordinating thread
- Sewing machine
- 45" x 60" (1.1 x 1.5m) white needled cotton batting (I recommend The Warm Company®)
- Lightweight tear-away stabilizer
- 10½" (26.7cm) square ruler
- Rotary cutter
- Terial Magic (optional)
- Owl design file (Owl.svg)

Prepare the Materials

1. Using your cutting machine software, upload the provided owl design file. Size your file to the appropriate size for your quilt. This design was built for a 10" (25.4cm) layer-cake square.

Decide which layer-cake fabric pieces you will use for your owls. The pattern uses two of each design, as shown, to make six owls total. Iron the fabric to release any creases or wrinkles. Using an iron, apply the double-sided fusible web to the back of each square that you have picked out for the main body, wing, and face features. Heat the fabric to the adhesive backing for approximately 10 to 15 seconds each; follow the manufacturer's recommendation for temperature. The adhesive backing should not peel from the fabric. Press again if necessary. **Note:** If you want a frayed edge appliqué, *do not* add fusible web at this point; instead, prepare squares with Terial Magic, following the instructions on page 40.

2. Following the settings on your selected cutter, load the fabric to your cutting mat. Use the brayer tool to make sure that your fabric has a firm hold on the mat. Not all machines have these settings. If your fabric is backed, use the bonded-fabric setting. Perform a test cut to check your settings. A good cut is one where the fabric and backing are cut cleanly with no loose threads.

TIP Make sure the owl pattern fits within the cut piece of fabric. It may be necessary to move the template around.

Make the Blocks

1. Audition your owls on the 10" (25.4cm) pre-cut squares to see which ones work the best for a background. If your cut pieces are already backed with fusible web, skip to step 2. If you are adding fusible web for a fringed edge, follow steps 1a–1c before moving to step 2.

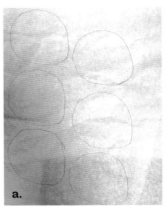
a.

b.

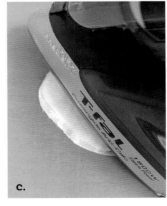
c.

a. Trace your owl and all the pieces each six times face down on the paper side of your adhesive web.

b. Cut a scant ¼" (0.6cm) inside the traced lines so your web pieces are slightly smaller than your owl pieces.

c. Center and apply the web to each piece according to the fusible web's directions. Let cool.

2. One square at a time, remove the paper backing from your web and position only the owl bodies onto the pre-selected blocks. Using a seam gauge, center each owl piece. Using an iron, adhere the owl body to the fabric block. Remember to press, not iron—do not move the iron back and forth. Remove the backing from the face piece and press it onto the head piece. Remove the backing from the eyes and beak, then press them onto the face to complete the head. Set the wings and prepared head pieces aside.

3. Once your owl body has cooled, take it to your sewing machine. Place it on top of a square of lightweight tear-away stabilizer, then straight-stitch anywhere from ⅛" to ¼" (0.3 to 0.6cm) inside the raw edge of the owl body. Don't worry about being precise; the beauty of raw-edge stitching is the primitive look. Go around the owl twice, crossing over stitch lines occasionally as shown. Repeat for all six owls.

4. Remove the backing from the prepared head and wing pieces. Position them onto the stitched owl body, using the photo of the finished owls on the quilt as a guide. Press to adhere.

5. Repeat these steps, one block at a time, until all six owl blocks are complete. Don't forget to place the block to be stitched on tear-away stabilizer. Carefully tear away the stabilizer after stitching.

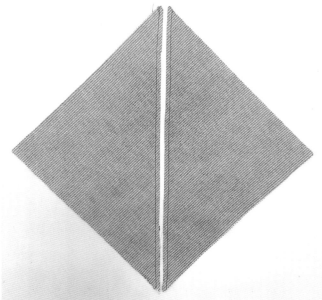

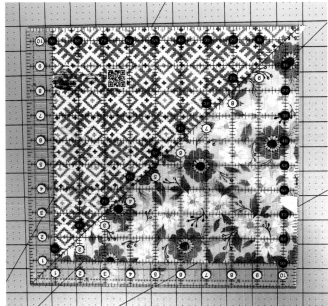

6. Use various combinations of the remaining 10" (25.4cm) layer-cake squares to make six half-square triangles. You can do this by either (1) cutting your 10" (25.4cm) squares in half diagonally and joining the halves with a ¼" (0.6cm) seam, or (2) placing two squares right sides together, drawing a diagonal line from corner to corner, stitching ¼" (0.6cm) on each side of the diagonal line, and then cutting on the diagonal line. **Note:** The second technique will yield two identical half-square triangles, but you need only one each of six different combinations.

7. Press all your owl and half-square triangle blocks. Use a square ruler and a rotary cutter to evenly trim all blocks to 9½" (24.1cm) square, making sure that the owls are centered.

Assemble the Quilt

ADDITIONAL CUTTING

- Four strips 1½" (3.8cm) x width of fabric (WOF) from Golden Gypsy, cut to center brown triangles in print, for narrow border
- Four strips 2¾" (7cm) x WOF from Skinny Stripes Olive Green for wide border
- 45" x 38" (1.1 x 1m) rectangle from Golden Gypsy for backing
- 2¼" (5.7cm)–wide strips from Golden Magic Dot, enough to make 164" (4.2m) of binding

1. Lay out your blocks in varying positions, three across and four down, until you're happy with the color and pattern placement.

2. Stitch together the blocks in each row, pressing the seams in opposite directions. Stitch each row together; press the seams up for rows 1 and 2 and down for rows 3 and 4.

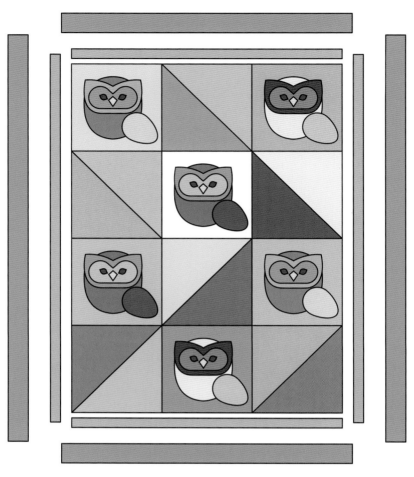

3. Referring to the quilt assembly diagram above, stitch the narrow border pieces to the top and bottom, press, and trim even with the sides. Join the remaining two narrow border pieces to the sides. Trim even with the top and bottom. Press. Join the wide border strips to the top and bottom and trim even with the sides. Join the remaining two border pieces to the sides. Press.

4. Layer the quilt top, batting, and backing, using quilt pins generously to keep them secure. Machine-stitch with a simple design in each half-square block, and machine-quilt a silhouette around each owl.

5. Finish with the polka dot binding. (See Binding Your Quilt on page 73.)

Binding Your Quilt

1. Fold the binding strip lengthwise in half. With raw edges aligned, start stitching your binding to the back side of the quilt edge, leaving at least 5" (12.7cm) of unstitched binding as a tail. As you approach the corner, stop stitching ¼" (0.6cm) before you reach the edge.

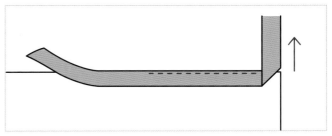

2. Backstitch to secure. Fold the binding up at a 90-degree angle.

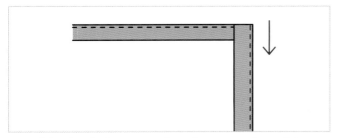

3. Fold it back down so that the raw edge of the binding is flush with the raw edge of the quilt/mat, and the top fold is aligned with the original side. Begin stitching where you left off on the previous side, making sure to fix your stitch line at the starting point. Continue around the quilt, stopping approximately 7" to 8" (17.8 to 20.3cm) from your starting point.

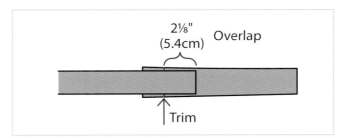

4. Lay the tails along the quilt edge so that they are smooth and flat. The overlap must be the same size as the width of your binding. Clip the excess ends of the tails perpendicular to the edge of the mat.

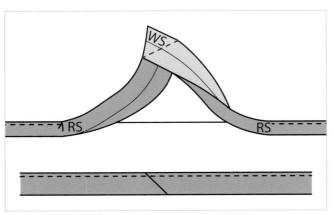

5. Place the ends right sides together at right angles. Stitch a diagonal line from corner to corner, then trim off the corner, leaving a ¼" (0.6cm) seam allowance. Now simply finger-press the binding into its original folded shape along the remaining raw edge of the mat. Press, pin, and continue stitching to secure, fixing your stitching line as you start and stop.

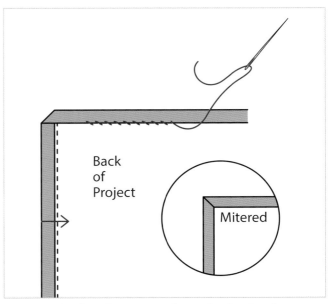

6. Press the binding away from the back edge and fold it over to the front of the quilt. Miter the binding at the corner and use your sewing machine to edge-stitch into place.

Felt-Lettered Pillows

Add a little designer pizzazz to a bedroom, dorm room, or family room. Use whatever words or message you want—even a name or nickname—to create a pillow cover with personality. The smaller letters are ideal for a 12" x 20" (30.5 x 50.8cm) pillow form. Larger letters can be applied in a square formation on a 20" x 20" (50.8 x 50.8cm) form. Include an invisible zipper opening, and you can switch out covers whenever you fancy a change.

MATERIALS AND TOOLS

Note: The following materials are used to create one 12" x 20" (30.5 x 50.8cm) pillow cover

- ¼ yard (22.9cm) felt in main color
- ¼ yard (22.9cm) felt in coordinating background color
- ½ yard (45.7cm) fabric for pillow front and back
- 2 yards (1.8m) trim for 12" x 20" (30.5 x 50.8cm) pillow (optional)
- Approximately ½ yard (45.7cm) Wonder-Under interfacing (or Heat n Bond fusible web)
- Polyester stuffing
- Fabric-tack cutting mat
- Light-grip cutting mat
- Fine-point blade
- Brayer tool
- Small scraper tool
- Small ironing board or mat
- Small piece of parchment paper
- Iron
- 12" x 20" (30.5 x 50.8cm) pillow form
- 10"–12" (25.4–30.5cm) invisible zipper (in coordinating color)
- Coordinating thread
- Water-soluble or air-soluble marking pen
- Seam gauge
- Fabric scissors or rotary cutter and ruler
- Sewing machine needle (I used Schmetz Microtex)
- Alphabet design file (Alphabet_Pillow.svg)

Prepare and Apply the Letters

1. Pick one of the words shown here or a word of your own, and choose the needed letters from the design file.

2. Size the letters according to the design and the space available on the pillow. The layered letters on the pillows shown are approximately 3⅝" (9.2cm) tall. The width varies by letter. **Tip:** In your software, create a rectangle the size of your pillow to help you determine the best size for your letters. This allows you to visualize how the letters will look on your pillow before cutting.

HOME

HOME

3. Once you are happy with the sizing, duplicate the entire project. This gives you a copy to cut out just for the adhesive backing. **Tip:** Setting the duplicate letters in white or gray will remind you that these need to be cut out with a more sensitive setting to protect the adhesive backing.

4. Following the instructions for your cutter, cut out the felt letters in your chosen colors.

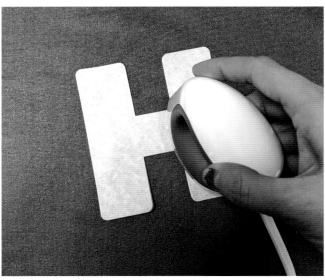

5. Once you've cut all your pieces, iron adhesive backing onto the back of each piece. For this process, set your iron to the wool setting.

6. Once you've ironed adhesive backing to every letter, attach the main felt color to the background color. Peel the paper backing off the adhesive iron-on letter and place it carefully onto your background color, shiny side down. Use a piece of parchment paper or a pressing cloth between the iron and the letter, then press gently over the lettering for five to ten seconds. Repeat with each letter in your design.

TIP If you don't want to cut out adhesive backing for every letter, attach the adhesive backing before you cut out your felt letters. You'll have more adhesive backing waste, but it is a nice shortcut!

Make the Pillow

Note: Seam allowances are ½" (1.3cm).

1. Trace the pillow front and back onto fabric with a fabric marking pen. The pieces should be 1" (2.5cm) larger than the pillow form, e.g., 13" x 21" (33 x 53.3cm) for a 12" x 20" (30.5 x 50.8cm) form.

2. Cut out the back piece and set it aside. Place the traced front piece on the ironing board and, taking into account the ½" (1.3cm) seam allowance, position your cut letters to create your word. Use a seam gauge to space the letters evenly and a ruler to make sure the letters will be centered from side to side and top to bottom. **Tip:** It's helpful to use a fabric marking pen to draw a straight line at the lower edge of the letters and to the side of each letter to serve as positioning guidelines.

3. Working one letter at a time, remove the paper backing and finger-press in place.

4. Lay a pressing cloth over the first letter and use an iron to set it in place, then turn it over and press without a pressing cloth on the back side.

TIP When positioning your word on the pillow, it helps to place the first and last letters first, then add the center letters to ensure even placement.

5. Thread your sewing machine with thread that matches the background letter felt. Slowly straight-stitch close to the edges around each letter silhouette. When the stitches meet, either cleanly backstitch or let the stitches meet, cut a top thread tail long enough to pull to the back side, and tie off with the bobbin thread. Repeat the stitching with thread in a color that matches the main letters.

6. Once your letters are topstitched in place, double-check the traced pillow front to make sure it is the correct size. Adjust if needed, then cut out the pillow front. For zipper installation, use a fabric marking pen to make a mark at the right side of the pillow front, and the left side of the pillow back 1½" (3.8cm) from the top and bottom and at the center point.

7. Optional: If adding piping or trim, place it so that you will apply it on a ½" (1.3cm) seam line on the pillow front. The tape of the trim will be on the cut edge, wrong side down, if your trim has a right and wrong side. The decorative part of the trim will be positioned toward the pillow center. Starting toward the bottom, on the left side of your pillow front, leave at least 3" (7.6cm) of piping/trim unstitched when you begin sewing. Stop just before your ½" (1.3cm) seam allowance at each corner, pivot your pillow, and continue sewing to form a soft corner with your trim.

Continue stitching around the pillow, stopping approximately 3" (7.6cm) before the starting point of your trim. Overlap the ends so that the tape falls at a slight angle out of the seam line, then pin. Finish stitching, keeping the decorative part of the trim in line.

 TIP A zipper foot allows you to stitch right where the decorative trim meets the trim tape; this also should be where your ½" (1.3cm) seam allowance hits.

Add a Hidden Zipper

A hidden zipper is a lovely option for a decorative pillow, especially if you have pets and might need to clean the covers. It also makes it easy to switch up the pillows for a fresh look: simply unzip, remove the insert from one cover, and use the insert with a different design. This technique can be used with or without applied trim.

1. Determine the size of your zipper by placing the zipper pull on the closed zipper at the 1½" (3.8cm) mark you made on the lower right side of your pillow front. You want your zipper stop (bottom) to be ½" (1.3cm) beyond the mark on the upper right side of your pillow (shown before trim applied).

2. Mark the placement of the zipper stop with a wash-away marking pen. If your zipper stop falls approximately at the right point, proceed to step 5. If you have a longer zipper, you'll need to create a zipper stop and cut off the excess.

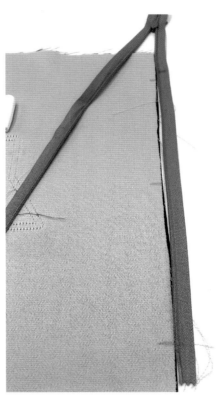

3. To create a zipper stop, set your machine for a 3.0- to 4.0-width zigzag (wide enough to stitch over the closed zipper coils) and a length of 0. Center the zipper under your presser foot and stitch back and forth several times over the coils at the stop point you marked in step 2.

4. Switch to a straight stitch, slide the zipper over so you're stitching on the zipper tape, and take a few stitches back and forth to secure the thread.

5. Remove from the machine and cut off the remaining zipper below your new stop, leaving at least 1" (2.5cm) of tape.

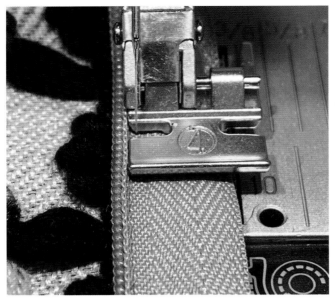

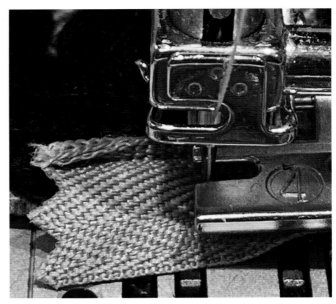

6. Unzip your zipper and flatten the tape with a warm iron. Place it face down on the right edge of your pillow front (shown with trim applied), so the left side coils align with the ½" (1.3cm) seam allowance line (the thread line that attached your trim), and the top plastic stop is 1½" (3.8cm) from the top. The pull should be against the bottom stop. Stitch close to the zipper teeth from the top to as close to the stop as you can. Secure your stitching with a back stich when you start and stop.

7. At the top of the zipper, stitch horizontally across the tape, above the stop, to secure the tape to the seam.

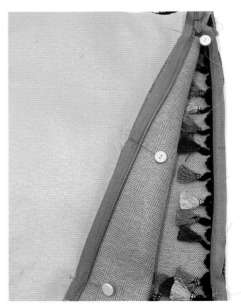

8. Zip up your zipper and position the front unit next to the pillow back. Using a wash-away marking pen, transfer the center mark across the zipper tape to ensure that the front and back pieces will match up once you've finished the zipper application.

9. Unzip the zipper and press the remining side flat. Pin the unattached side of the zipper face down to the right side of the opposite pillow piece so the center marks align. Stitch close to the zipper coils as you did to apply the first side, starting and stopping at the same points.

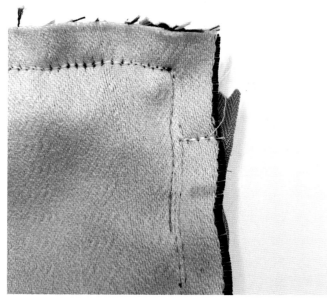

10. Zip up the zipper again so that the pillow front and back are right sides together. Stitch the pillow together at the top and bottom of the zipper, starting at the 1½" (3.8cm) mark and ⅛" (0.3cm) outside the line you stitched to apply the zipper and around the corner a bit. You want to stitch close to that previous stitch line but not so close that you stitch through the zipper (the image shows the wrong side of stitching). When the top and bottom are joined above and below the zipper, unzip the zipper.

11. Place the pillow front and back right sides together and finish stitching around the pillow with a ½" (1.3cm) seam allowance. If you applied trim, you'll be stitching directly over that same line of stitching.

12. Turn the pillow right side out through the zipper opening. Stuff with a pillow form and zip closed.

Holiday Ornaments

Creating your own vintage felt ornaments is easy with the help of your digital cutter. This twist on a classic can be customized for any age or occasion. Add beads and sequins, and a bit of batting for dimension, and finish with a blanket stitch. **Note:** While the step-by-step photos show the mitten ornament, you can follow the same steps to complete the tree and gift ornaments pictured below.

MATERIALS AND TOOLS

- Felt in 2 or 3 colors of your choice
- Ribbon to hang the ornament
- Sequins, bugle beads, and seed beads
- 1 sheet white HTV
- Embroidery floss (I used DMC) in matching or contrasting colors
- Clear sewing thread
- Embroidery needle
- Beading needle
- Basting glue
- Approximately 2–3 oz. polyester fill
- Pressing cloth (**Note:** Always use a pressing cloth when using an iron on felt.)
- Ornament design file (Gift Box.svg, Mitten.svg, or Tree.svg)

1. Upload the SVG file of one of the ornaments. Select both pieces and create a duplicate. The images show the separated files and joined final image. You can make your ornament any size you wish; these examples finished between 6"–7" (15.2–17.8cm).

2. Cut out the pieces for your ornament. The mitten is cut from red felt with white HTV for the iron-on snowflake and white felt for the cuff overlay. The tree is cut from green felt with brown felt for the stem overlay. The gift is cut from green felt for the package with red felt for the ribbon and bow overlay.

3. If making the mitten, center and iron your snowflake decal onto the mitten front using a pressing cloth or parchment paper. For the gift or tree ornament, use basting glue to add the felt accents. Use clear thread and a beading needle to add decorative beading: seed beads and bugle beads embellish the mitten, seed beads and sequins decorate the tree to represent ornaments, and all three types of beads decorate the gift. Add embellishments to the back ornament piece if desired.

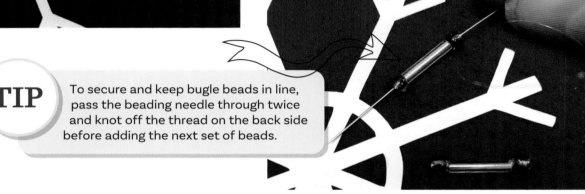

TIP To secure and keep bugle beads in line, pass the beading needle through twice and knot off the thread on the back side before adding the next set of beads.

TIP To keep your blanket stitch nice and even, set your sewing machine to a 6.0 basting stitch and sew between ⅛"–¼" (0.3–0.6cm) from the edge on the front ornament piece only. Repeat for one cuff piece.

4. Layer together the front and back pieces. Using an embroidery needle and embroidery floss, work a blanket stitch around the sides of the ornament, starting in the right "corner" below where you will apply the cuff. Stitch through all layers, following the blanket stitch as a guide.

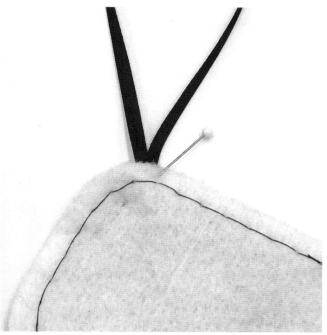

5. Piece the ornament together. When you work all the way around the mitten to the left cuff "corner," pin on the front and back cuff pieces over the cuff area of the mitten. You could also secure the pieces with a few small dots of basting glue.

6. Place a piece of ribbon loop in between the front and back mitten pieces of your ornament. The ribbon should be about 4" to 6" (10.2 to 15.2cm) long. Pin or glue-baste in place.

TIP Use sewing pins or clips to hold the ornament in place while sewing the back and front together.

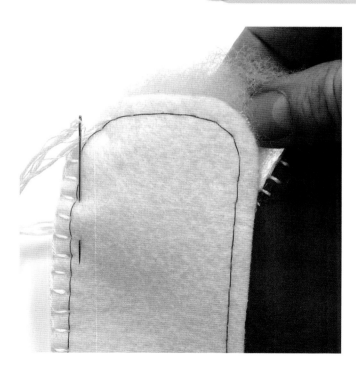

7. Continue blanket-stitching around the cuff, catching the loop. Stop stitching at the right side of the cuff, then slip some polyester stuffing into the opening to add dimension to the mitten. Distribute the stuffing to fill the ornament. **Note:** The ornament shown does not have filling in the cuff area, but you can choose to fill the entire ornament.

Faux-Suede Hexagonal Pillow

Sensuede® is a win-win fabric for digital cutting. It not only cuts like a breeze, but quality fabric-weight suedes won't ravel, so you can leave a clean raw edge without any stabilizers, seam sealants, or webbing. This hexagon pillow project adds rich detail to the décor of any room, yet it is incredibly simple to make. Make as many small hexagons as you want and arrange them however you like. You can even use more than two colors. The options are endless.

MATERIALS AND TOOLS

- ⅝ yard (57.2cm) Sensuede in Deep Turquoise
- ⅓ yard (30.5cm) Silky Sensuede in Serpentine (dark blue)
- Brayer tool
- Fabric or strong-tack mat
- Rotary blade
- Fabric scissors

- 18" (45.7cm) square pillow form
- 20"–22" (50.8–55.9cm) invisible zipper in coordinating color
- Temporary basting glue (I used Roxanne Glue-Baste-It®)
- Thread in coordinating colors

- Chalk marker or wash-away fabric marker
- Erasable pen (I used a Clover Eraser Pen) and straightedge
- Hexagon design file (Hexagon Pillow.svg or Hexagon Pillow2.svg)

Prepare the Hexagons

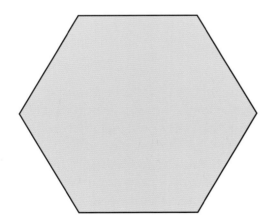

1. Use your design software to upload the hexagon SVG. Duplicate the image to cut approximately 25 hexagons of each color.

TIP If any of your hexagons don't cut through all the way, finish cutting with fabric scissors. Use the lines on the fabric as a guide.

2. Place the suede on the mat. Use a brayer tool to firmly press the fabric on the mat, making sure the fabric is flat and smooth. This is a good project for the rotary blade, but a regular blade works great too.

Make the Pillow

1. Trace two 19" (48.3cm) squares on your turquoise yardage. Cut one for the pillow back and set aside.

2. Start positioning the small hexagons on the pillow front, making sure that they are all at least 1½" (3.8cm) from the traced lines of your pillow front. Position as many of the hexagons as you want until you're happy with the design.

3. One by one, drop a dot or a narrow horizontal line of glue baste under each hexagon and finger-press back into place. Let dry.

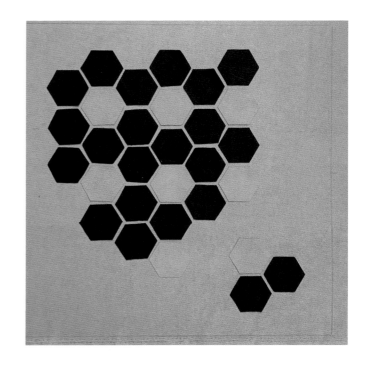

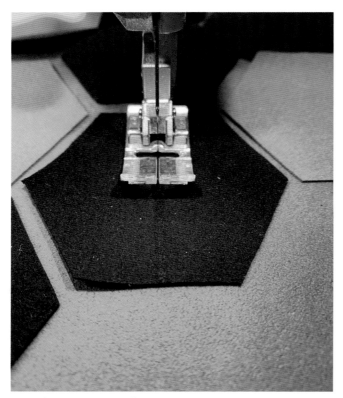

TIP To ensure straight stitching when attaching the hexagons, keep a small straightedge and an erasable pen next to your machine and mark your sewing line one by one as you stitch. The eraser pen leaves a light temporary mark that is easy to follow and disappears before you're on to the next hexagon.

4. Take the pillow front to your machine. With thread colors that match the hexagons, straight-stitch through the center of each hexagon, backstitching two or three stitches at the start and stop of each hexagon.

5. Once all your hexagons are attached, thread any long tails through a hand-sewing needle and pull them through to the back side.

6. Pair the pillow front with the pillow back. Refer to Add a Hidden Zipper on page 79 to finish your pillow.

Drawstring Gift Bags

Drawstring bags are easy to come by, but it's so much easier to make your own for pennies on the dollar in any size or fabric you'd like. You can then add cute designs to your finished bags for any purpose or occasion. See page 13 for information on adding the designs shown to your bags. **Note:** In the instructions, the stitching is in a contrasting thread color for easier visibility.

MATERIALS AND TOOLS

- ⅓ yard (30.5cm) muslin or lightweight canvas fabric
- 1 yard (91.4cm) rope trim
- Thread to match
- Design file (Birthday Cake.svg or Bunnies.svg)

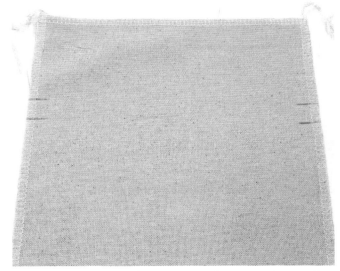

2. On the wrong side, measure down 3" (7.6cm) from one short end and make a mark ⅝" (1.6cm) long for the drawstring opening. Repeat on the opposite side.

1. Cut a rectangle 27.5" long x 9.5" wide (69.9 x 24.1cm) and finish the edges with a zigzag stitch or serger.

3. Fold the bag in half, right sides together, and stitch down the sides, stopping and starting and securing the stitches on each side of the ⅝" (1.6cm) mark.

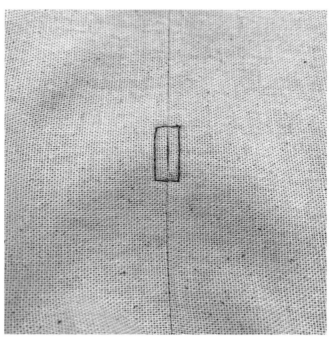

4. Press open the seams.

5. On the right side, stitch a small rectangle around the opening left in the seam.

6. Fold the top edge to the wrong side ¼" (0.6cm), then 1⅞" (4.8cm) to form a casing; edge-stitch to secure. Then stitch a second row of topstitching in the center of casing. Make sure your second line of stitching is above your tie opening. Turn right side out.

7. Weave an 18" (45.7cm) length of rope though the opening in the left side of the back, around, and back out the same opening. Repeat for the right-side opening. Tie off each rope in a clean knot.

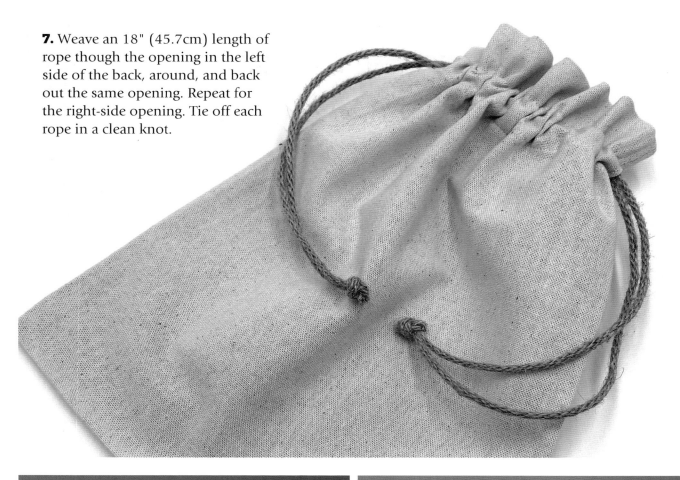

Index

Photo Credits

Libby Ashcraft, 44-45, 47, 48 (bottom), 49 (top), 52-57, 62-65, 68-70, 74, 76-81, 84-86, 88 (bottom), 89 (bottom), 90, 92-93

David Fisk, 10, 46 (top)

Mike Mihalo, 2, 5, 8-13, 18, 41 (bottom), 43 (inset), 46 (bottom left and right), 48 (top), 49, 50 (top), 51 (bottom), 58, 61, 67, 75, 83, 87, 88 (top), 91

Chanti Sprauve, Personal Vision Photography, page 96

Courtesy of Shutterstock: Mayboroda Alexander, 38; coasehsieh, 16; EugeniaSt, 42; Evgeniya369, 40; Arina P Habich, 50 (bottom); hernantron, 14; Mira Kos, 41 (top); Lili.Q, 43 (background); Kostikova Natalia, 4, 36; New Africa, 39; Nurul Shafiqah Nsf, 17, 51 (top); Diego Diaz Piedra, 37; Tada Images, 31; Vladitto (white wood background), 5, 61, 67, 75, 83, 87, 91

Courtesy of Silhouette America, 7

Illustrations pages 22-23, 26-27, 32-35 by Winnifred Casacop

Illustrations pages 66, 71-73 by Sue Friend

Acknowledgments

Thanks so much to my husband, Joe, for his patience and support with this book and all my other crafting endeavors. Special thanks to my "supervisors" Dixie Belle and Skye for reminding me to take time to play. And thanks to my grandson JD for his understanding when I say, "Grandma has to work."

About the Author

Libby Ashcraft has been teaching sewing, embroidery, and embroidery software for more than twenty years. Libby is a Terri Johnson Creates Licensed Silhouette Instructor and teaches the Silhouette Cameo at workshops and classes around the country. She also teaches Brother ScanNCut classes, providing interactive and informative lessons for her students. As a Martha Pullen Licensed Teacher, Libby travels the United States to bring the joy of sewing to many students, and she is also a teaching assistant at Martha Pullen licensing courses. Libby has presented at All Things Silhouette, Appliqué Getaway, and Original Sewing and Quilting Expo events. In addition to her teaching, Libby is a technical sewing editor and contributor for *Classic Sewing* magazine.

Libby lives in Texas with her husband of forty-three years. They have two sons, four grandchildren, and two dogs, Dixie Belle and Skye.

How to contact me:

Email: *libby@libbyashcraft.com*
Facebook: *www.facebook.com/LibbysLoftTX*
Facebook group: Libby's Craft and Sewing Group
Facebook group: Libby's Silhouette Group—
Tips, Tricks, Tutorials and Projects